Black
Fiction

Black Fiction

Roger Rosenblatt

Harvard University Press
Cambridge, Massachusetts, and London, England

Publication of this book has been aided by a grant
from the Andrew W. Mellon Foundation

Library of Congress Catalog Card Number 74–81387
ISBN 0–674–07620–6 (cloth)
ISBN 0–674–07622–2 (paper)
Printed in the United States of America

For Mom and Dad,
Ginny, Carl, and Amy

Acknowledgments

In the fall of 1968, Harlon Dalton, John Tyson, Chuck Hamilton, and a number of other black undergraduates in Harvard College encouraged my teaching a formal course in black American literature. I wish to thank them for that, for enhancing my understanding of the material, and for initiating the interest which led to this book.

I am very grateful to Harvard University for the leave of absence during which most of this book was finished; and to the National Endowment for the Humanities and the Canaday Fund of the Harvard Faculty of Arts and Sciences for their fellowship grants in support of this project.

I am much indebted to Barbara Stone, who, piece by piece, saw to the preparation of the manuscript; to Karen DeGraffenreid, who attended to many essential typing and bibliographical chores; and to Nancy Clemente, who has edited the manuscript with great care. To the relentless Maud Wilcox, Editor-in-Chief of Harvard University Press, I owe the book's completion.

I have been immensely helped by the guidance and criticism of the text offered by Dr. Ronald S. Berman, Chairman of the National Endowment for the Humanities; Professor Sterling A. Brown of Howard University; Ralph Ellison; Dr. O. B. Hardison, Director of the Folger Shakespeare Library; Professor Irving Howe of Hunter College of the City University of New York; Professor Lucio Ruotolo of Stanford University; Professors Alan E. Heimert, Harry Levin, and James Q. Wilson of Harvard University.

My gratitude for the wisdom and kindness of these people, and for that of present and former teachers at Harvard, Professors William Alfred, Herschel Baker, W. J. Bate, Morton Bloomfield, Walter Kaiser, John V. Kelleher, and John L. Sweeney is deep and abiding.

I also thank the following friends for their aid and advice: William Alexander of the University of Michigan, Phillip L. Marcus of Cornell University, Arnold Rampersad of Stanford University, Alan Weinblatt of Boston College, Philip M. Weinstein of Swarthmore College, and Terry M.

Krieger and Rhona Ready of the National Endowment for the Humanities.

My thanks, above all, to my wife, Ginny, for the love and sense she brought to every stage of this work.

I am grateful to Harper & Row and Jonathan Cape Ltd. for permission to quote from Richard Wright's *Native Son*, Copyright 1940 by Richard Wright, and to Harper & Row for quotations from Wright's *Uncle Tom's Children*, Copyright 1936, 1937, 1938 by Richard Wright, renewed 1964, 1965, 1966 by Ellen Wright; to Hope McKay Virtue for permission to quote from Claude McKay's *Home to Harlem*; to The Dial Press for permission to quote from James Baldwin's *Another Country*, Copyright © 1960, 1962 by James Baldwin, and Baldwin's *Go Tell It on the Mountain*, Copyright 1952, 1953 by James Baldwin; to Alfred A. Knopf, Inc., for permission to quote from James Weldon Johnson's *The Autobiography of an Ex-Colored Man*, Copyright 1927 by Alfred A. Knopf, Inc., renewal Copyright 1955 by Carl Van Vechten, and from Langston Hughes's *Not Without Laughter*, Copyright 1930 by Alfred A. Knopf, Inc.; to Liveright Publishing Corporation for permission to quote from Jean Toomer's *Cane*, Copyright 1923 by Boni & Liveright, Inc., Copyright renewed 1951 by Jean Toomer; to J. B. Lippincott Company for permission to quote from Zora Neale Hurston's *Their Eyes Were Watching God*, Copyright 1937 by J. B. Lippincott Company, Copyright © renewed 1965 by John C. Hurston and Joel Hurston; to Macmillan Publishing Company and Jonathan Cape Ltd. for permission to quote from Claude Brown's *Manchild in the Promised Land*, Copyright © 1965 by Claude Brown; to Dodd, Mead & Company for permission to quote from Paul Laurence Dunbar's *The Uncalled*; to Doubleday & Company, Inc., for permission to quote from William M. Kelley's *dem*, Copyright © 1964, 1967 by William Melvin Kelley; to the Roslyn Targ Literary Agency, Inc., for permission to quote from Chester Himes's *If He Hollers Let Him Go*, Copyright 1945 by Chester B. Himes; to Houghton Mifflin Company for permission to quote from Ann Petry's *Country Place*; to Beacon Press and Michael Joseph Ltd., for permission to quote from James Baldwin's *Notes of a Native Son*; and to Random House, Inc., for permission to quote from Ralph Ellison's *Invisible Man*, Copyright 1947, 1952 by Ralph Ellison.

R.R.

Contents

Black
Fiction

Introduction

Despite occasional periods of popularity, black fiction has encouraged a surprisingly small amount of literary criticism over the years. What criticism there has been of the material has primarily been involved with questions deriving from the subject as subject, and not with its contents. The most recurrent questions, which go back to William Stanley Braithwaite and Benjamin Brawley, among the first to consider this literature, are: (1) Should black authors address themselves solely to the conditions of black life in America or to a wider, or international range of subjects? (2) Who is better equipped to judge the quality of these books, a black critic or a white one? (3) Is social protest the only proper aim and theme of black writers? (4) Is it right (sensible, fair) to talk about black fiction as a genre or only to discuss individual novels, short stories, and authors? (5) Is black fiction a genuine subject, separable from modern American fiction as a whole? Important as all of these questions are, only the last two, those involving if or how one treats the subject generally, are problems in literary criticism. The others concern literature as social argument, and when observers such as Addison Gayle, Jr., Nick Aaron Ford, William Gardner Smith, and Julian Mayfield have raised them, they have done so more for purposes of social than literary comment.

The two remaining questions have their own social applications, but they are essential to any analysis of the literature as well because one's decisions about them set up the frames of reference in which all other and more specific observations either make sense or do not. The question of whether one ought to deal with the overall subject of black fiction instead of taking up each author separately is the easier problem to handle because it leads to a middle ground. There are critics who urge us not to generalize about black writing because that might obscure the diversity of the material, and there are others who suggest that black literature is so much of a piece that it has its own aesthetic. The second point of view is not true, as I believe

1

an investigation of the characteristics of the literature proves, and the first diminishes much of the importance of the subject. Yes, there is diversity in black fiction, but there also are discernible norms and pattterns which have been common to black fiction from 1890 to the present, the detection of which in no way undermines the individualities of the writers.

As for the specialness of the subject within the larger context of American fiction, part of the case has already been made effectively by Robert A. Bone, Horace Cayton, Charles I. Glicksberg, J. Saunders Redding (although Redding warns about making the distinction too severe), by Langston Hughes, Richard Wright, and others: that the experience of black people in America, for all its diversity and exceptions, has been a unique and insular experience, and that therefore the novels and short stories which depict that experience have also been special and have stood on their own. The point to emphasize, the point on which this book depends, and from which it departs, is not only that there has been a correspondence between the experiences and the various stories, but that the stories have been similar to each other as well, that indeed, while a number of literary movements and digressions was occurring in the nation at large over the past eighty years, black fiction has continued to function within patterns peculiarly its own. It is the existence of the patterns, not simply of common external experiences, which makes the subject real.

Observers of the wider scope of American literature, notably Richard Chase (*The American Novel and Its Tradition*), have cited and emphasized two defining aspects of the product: the "extreme range of experience" (Chase) carried in the novels, and particularly the number and size of the unresolved contradictions. In American black fiction one does not find the first characteristic at all, and one only finds the second in a different form. Although black stories often end in unresolved contradictions, the overriding sense of contradiction does not reside within the main characters or events, but is attached to the situation, ordinarily white and middle class, in which the characters function and events take place. The heroes and heroines of the literature may have their personal contradictions, but these are usually subsumed in, and overwhelmed by, the enormous contradictions posed by the world outside.

This is not to say that the tragedies which occur in this arrangement are merely the modern tragedies of victimization. It is true that much of each main character's mental and sometimes physical energy is spent in his relationship to a callous or evil society which always wins; but as a literary figure, he is not delineated by the frictions inherent in that relationship as much as by the fact that the peculiar conditions, and usually the intense moments, of his situation have caused him to examine or search for those interior elements of character of which classical heroism might be made. Bob Jones, for example, of Chester Himes's *If He Hollers Let Him Go*, both is paranoid and has real enemies. His eventual stature is born not superficially or cheaply, of the effort to identify his proper place in the conspiring world, but of the desire to quash within himself the flaw of personality which keeps victory away.

Where resolutions of various contradictions have been attempted in American novels generally, as Chase points out, these attempts have been made either by means of moral equivocation, melodrama, the pastoral impulse, humor, or one or another form of abstraction. It is largely because of these abstractions that the American novel has been characterized as a romance. The black American novel, however, is not a romance, although it almost always contains romantic elements, primarily because it lacks the tendency toward abstraction. Not that massive struggles between light and dark, good and evil, and so on, do not occur in black fiction—indeed, they do so in particularly terrifying ways—but they occur at a level which makes abstraction unnecessary, and even preposterous. Unlike other American literary heroes, black heroes are not pioneers. They may believe that they control their own destinies, but they rarely do; most of the time, The Whale seeks them.

It is not true, however, that because black fiction has

been separable from the rest of American literature it has also been independent of it. Themes which have been ascribed as characteristically American—themes of the wilderness and frontier, of the effects of a forceful religion on the individual mind, of the explorations of actual and psychological terror, of the quests for personal and national freedom, romance, cultural security—are the themes of black fiction as well. Stock American literary figures such as the confidence man and Yankee peddler show up in black fiction too, as do celebrations of the outlaw, the outcast, and versions of the standard American success story. The loose structure of black novels simulates the loose structure of American novels as a whole. The problem of national self-definition which has regularly dominated American writers is at the heart of black fiction. The choice of the novel over poems and plays as the predominant means of expression is itself a typically American choice.

Invariably the examples of dependency tend to sharpen the distinctions. Richard Wright's conception of horror is not Brockden Brown's or Poe's, nor is his naturalism that of Norris or Dreiser. The power of Christianity in James Baldwin is much different from that in Hawthorne. Claude McKay's primitive is not Cooper's, nor is John Williams' expatriot adventurer like those of Hemingway or James. Jean Toomer creates his own kind of solitary wanderer. The families which disintegrate in Ann Petry and Zora Neale Hurston are unlike their counterparts in Cable or Faulkner. Langston Hughes's Simple is cut from the same mold as Josh Billings and Mr. Dooley, but he is different from either. Claude Brown's narrator talks like Ben Franklin, but he has another kind of wisdom to offer. Ralph Ellison's Rinehart and William Kelley's Cooley are con men as shifty as Melville's and Twain's, but they pull different tricks for different reasons.

In spite of such differences, the general characteristics of American writing have been essential to black fiction in a special way. Whatever American literature may consist of in terms of individual accomplishments, it has been since its beginnings a general expression of how people deal with personal, spiritual, social, economic, and political freedom in the new world. In a sense, this has also been what black fiction has expressed since it came into being, but in its instance the fullness of the freedom has been modified by the conditions of the immediate past. Moreover, the new world was not the black man's by choice. If, since 1860, it has been the same new world that the black and white writer have regarded, they have not regarded it from the same perspectives. The American literary conventions which have been suited to black writing have therefore provided something to lean on and push against at the same time. In most cases they have served as instruments of criticism, every American theme, idea, and figure used in black fiction inevitably probing and scrutinizing the model it reflects.

This operation of criticism, as Wright and LeRoi Jones have pointed out, has been an integral part of black writing even from its earliest and most benign statements, and has been directed at conceptions of the national character as well as the national literature. Jones ("Philistinism and the Negro Writer") describes the operation in terms of a man (black) who has been locked up in one room of a large house by another man (white) who never enters that room. When the isolated man finally comes out, says Jones, he is able to talk about the whole house, whereas the man who imprisoned him is not. The argument implied is that the black writer may be more fit to handle the totality of America in his work than a white one. Whether or not this is so, the freed man (artist), having been locked up, is bound to serve as a critic of both the jailer and the jail. Even in the process of determining who or what he has become, he must understand where he has been, why he has been there, and who put him there in the first place.

Wright said that "the Negro is America's metaphor" ("The Literature of the Negro in the United States"), meaning that whatever spirit of decency and courage may originally have inspired the founding of the nation, having since been perverted, now resides, if incubatively, in the black man who has borne the brunt of that perversion. If it is true that the Negro is America's metaphor, the reverse is also true, at least for the black writer. Images and ideas of America or of what has been called the promise of America are at the core of black fiction. The oppressive elements in American life which have been recorded and transformed into art have created a literary tradition of their own. Contemporary black critics such as Larry Neal and Hoyt Fuller contend that this tradition has been inadequate and stifling, that it has locked the black writer into a perpetual relationship with white American life which has dulled his imagination. Yet nothing in the work of Toomer, Wright, Himes, Petry, Hurston, Baldwin, Ellison, Paule Marshall, Williams, Hal Bennet, Kelley, and others suggests that this dulling has occurred. As painful and bitter as the feelings have been which have gone into the relationship between black writers and the country as a whole, the relationship has continued to support a valuable literary framework, a framework as defined and rigid as any Elizabethan framework, in which black writers have tested and elaborated upon their powers of invention within and because of certain restrictions.

The urgency and intensity which many critics, black and white, have shown in pressing black writers to find their own separate and unique forms and symbols tend to obscure the fact that these forms and symbols have existed all along. The subject matter of black fiction is not wide but it is very deep, and it has deepened and solidified with each successful exploration. In a sense, the modern American black writer has had an advantage denied to most other modern writers in that he has had a consistent and built-in mythology to draw on, one formed out of difficult and often ugly and brutal elements, and one in which the gods frequently behave as demons, but a mythology nevertheless. Ironically, the general cruelty of black life in America has been something to believe in, a faith.

One of the telling, if obvious, facts about this literature is that it runs the full course of its history within what we know as the modern literary period. Except for the stories of William Wells Brown, Frank Webb, Martin Delany, and Charles Chesnutt, and not counting the slave narratives of Briton Hammon, John Marrant, Gustavus Vassa, Frederick Douglass, Solomon Bayley, and others, which are not properly works of fiction, all black fiction of significance in America is modern fiction, and what we expect of modernism in general, we expect of this literature as well: complexity of expression, elusiveness of meaning, opposition to established and traditional systems, social and aesthetic, a tendency toward fragmentation, elements of violence, a certain self-consciousness of modernity itself, and particularly the preeminence of subjectivity, which takes shape in a sense of loss and dislocation on the part of major characters. To one or another degree, most of these expectations are satisfied. Until recently there has been little complexity of expression in black fiction, but fragmentation has often been used as a method of presentation, and anti-societal themes predominate in the literature, as do acts of violence.

The "modern" attribute which is not displayed in the literature, that is, not displayed in the anti-heroic form commonly associated with modernism, is the subjective element. To be sure, all black heroes are underdogs, but so are twentieth-century heroes in general, and except for charting degrees of comparative failure it would be very difficult to draw a theoretical distinction between the sets of black and white losers in the modern novel. What distinguishes the black character's situation is not that he is oppressed, but that a great part of the nature of his oppression is prescribed by a physical characteristic. Because of his color the black character is denied full underdog privileges. All manifestations of self-indulgence enjoyed by his white counterparts are tempered in him and set apart. The white hero has the luxury of celebrating his own frailty, but the black hero does not. His ordinary human failings, his guilt or sense of loneliness or madness, are persistently undermined by the fact of his minority. And his struggles, unlike those of Dostoevsky's heroes, or of Kafka's, Mann's, Fitzgerald's, or Hemingway's, are directed not at reaching a point where he can begin to recognize his own manhood, but at reaching a specific kind of manhood which has been dictated by history.

No black hero ever gets all the way through his story without perceiving at least once and significantly that he is despicable or frightening to the white world or to himself, or that he is lost or isolated. If at such moments he thinks metaphorically, he almost always does so in images of darkness. If he or his author is merely describing events or circumstance, the same images recur. Baldwin christened his first hero Grimes (*Go Tell It on the Mountain*):

> he struggled to flee—out of this darkness, out of this company—into the land of the living, so high, so far away. Fear was upon him, a more deadly fear than he had ever known, as he turned and turned in the darkness, as he moaned, and stumbled, and crawled through darkness, finding no hand, no voice, finding no door. *Who are these? Who are they?* They were the despised and rejected, the wretched and the spat upon, the earth's off-scouring; and he was in their company, and they would swallow up his soul. (273)

In *Native Son* Wright's Bigger Thomas moved "ensnared in a tangle of deep shadows, shadows as black as the night that stretched above his head" (72).

> Standing trembling in his cell, he saw a dark vast fluid image rise and float; he saw a black sprawling prison full of tiny black cells in which people lived; each cell had its stone jar of water and a crust of bread and no one could go from cell to cell and there were screams and curses and yells of suffering and nobody heard them, for the walls were thick and darkness was everywhere. (334–335)

In Wright's *Uncle Tom's Children* Mann's body "seemed encased in a tight vise, in a narrow black coffin that moved with him as he moved" (223). Sarah has a nightmare:

> when she strained to see who it was that was pulling her no one was in sight but far ahead was darkness and

it seemed that out of the darkness some force came
and pulled her like a magnet and she went sliding over
a rough bed of screeching shucks and it seemed that
a wild fear made her want to scream but when she
opened her mouth to scream she could not scream and
she felt she was coming to a wide black hole and again
she made ready to scream and then it was too late for
she was already over the wide black hole falling falling
falling . . . (204)

When Johnson's Ex-Colored Man (*The Autobiography of
an Ex-Colored Man*) witnesses the burning of a black man
at the stake, his response to the "blackened bones" is
neither anger nor revulsion, but shame and humiliation. In
Not Without Laughter, when Hughes's Harriet was a child
the white boys danced "round and round her and yelling:
'Blackie! Blackie! Blackie!' while she screamed and tried
to run away. But they held her and pulled her hair terribly,
and her friends laughed because she *was* black and she *did*
look funny" (83). In Toomer's *Cane*, Esther, who looks
white, dreams she claims a baby whom she rescues from a
fire. "The women scoot in all directions from the danger
zone. She alone is left to take the baby in her arms. But
what a baby! Black, singed, wooly, tobacco-juice baby—
ugly as sin" (41). John, the theater manager's brother, wants
Dorris, one of the dancers. John is ashamed of being black,
and at the end of her rehearsal Dorris looks at him: "His
whole face is in shadow. She seeks for her dance in it. She
finds it a dead thing in the shadow which is his dream,"
and "cries bitterly" (99, 100). Paul, who is passing for white,
loves a white girl, Bona. He is "rosy before his window. He
moves, slightly, towards Bona. With his own glow, he seeks
to penetrate a dark pane" (147). In every instance black is
synonymous with rejection, defeat, impossibility, or some
aspect of a predetermined life. Black is both the color the
hero bears and the force against which he pits his strength.
    It is specifically this acknowledgment of external
limitation and the anticipation of it which distinguishes
black fiction within modern literature, and brings it close
to classical tragedy. Here color, the condition of darkness,

becomes fate. Within it or attached to it are all the forces necessary for the predetermination of a story or a career, and despite the apparent "modernity," the introspective nature, of the various battles waged in the literature, each of them boils down to the simple, if devastating, conflict between human and superhuman power. The tension in the literature derives from the anticipation of a fall caused by the alignment of a personal disability with an external circumstance. The circumstance in question is blackness itself, which carries with it enough cultural prejudgments to make the vengeance of a god seem meager.

The essence of tragedy, as George Steiner has pointed out (in *The Death of Tragedy*), is that it is irreparable, not merely irreparable from the viewpoint of the protagonist, but provably so, in objective reality. If any body of modern literature may be said to possess such a quality, it is black fiction. The scope of individual capacity with which we associate classical heroism, and the scope of mass oppression with which we associate modern heroism are conjoined in black fiction, but are not in balance, and in our apprehension of both forces, the advantage always swings to the outside element because its authenticity is proven by historical events. The key to tragedy is our feeling, upon witnessing a character's disintegration, that it must be so, that it could have been no other way. That is the feeling this literature conveys, from which it takes its power, and its form.

In an essay written for *Commentary* in 1947, "The Legacy of the 30's," Robert Warshow asked, "How shall we regain the use of our experience in the world of mass culture?" The question implies an essential modern problem, because it ultimately tests the compatibility of culture and democracy. Black fiction in America has emerged totally within a world of mass culture, and yet it has neither been a product of mass culture nor contained those elements which put such a culture at odds with art. It has not lacked the particularity on which art depends, and which is absent in most of modern fiction, nor has it overreached itself in order to make various "universal" statements. Whatever "universal" statements are detectable in *The Outsider* and *Invisible Man* are only "universal" insofar as they apply to all black men living in urban North America since the turn of the century. These books, and a few others like them which deal principally in symbolic circumstances, may make their appeal to a world of mass culture, but are themselves grounded in a specific culture and specific instances.

The basic paradox in this is that if black fiction has supported a single dominant theme over the years, that theme has been the search for a grounding or cultural history, that is, the search for the very condition which called it into being from the start. To pursue the paradox, the widely agreed-upon, almost institutionalized, absence of a full-length and long-reaching black cultural tradition has served as a substitute for the presence of such a tradition; and if the substitute has been a poor one, it has nevertheless provided enough community of experience to reduce the banalities which ordinarily attend the universalizing impulse. Even the closing question of *Invisible Man*—"Who knows but that, on the lower frequencies, I speak for you?"—is not the usual modern appeal. The qualification "on the lower frequencies" applies to a particular people, time, and place.

What we have, then, in black fiction is a literature both American and anti- or extra-American, modern and anti-modern, in sum, a body of writing not usefully classifiable except by the kind and number of the things it is not. In fact, without meaning to sound perverse, it may be said that modern black fiction in America is not only not typically modern or American, it is not purely fiction. So much of this literature is autobiographical (*Not Without Laughter, Their Eyes Were Watching God, Go Tell It on the Mountain*), so much of the autobiography, fictional (*Manchild in the Promised Land, Black Boy*), that the genres are largely interchangeable. Ordinarily this would place a certain burden on the reader in that he would wonder how to view such work as art. The question rarely occurs, however, because the events and circumstances of the stories are so extraordinary and nightmarish, no matter how true to life, that the literature seems to be not only fiction but fantasy, indeed, to be what it is, the depiction of a world removed.

Histories of black fiction usually divide the subject into four movements: the assimilationist or apologist period before World War I; the period of the Harlem Renaissance, in which black authors celebrated rather than concealed or adjusted their cultural identity; the period of the protest literature, which came to a head in the years during the Depression and carried forward through the mid-forties; and the most recent era, which is probably too diffuse and close to us to be categorized accurately. There may be another break between black fiction of the fifties and thereafter, but the line of demarcation is hard to spot because of the current shift from fiction to nonfiction. Moreover, as wide-ranging and experimental as the most recent writing is, it has so many elements of the old Harlem Renaissance in it that we may only be seeing a renaissance reborn, not the emergence of a new era.

The existence of these distinguishable movements would seem to indicate that there has been a linear progression in black fiction, and that the unity of the subject derives from the fact that its various changes of direction have grown out of each other logically. Accounts of this chronological unity have already been given in detail in earlier full-length studies of the subject, notably Robert A. Bone's *The Negro Novel in America* and Carl M. Hughes's *The Negro Novelist*. The following discussion differs from those earlier works. It seeks to show that the unity in black fiction has little to do with chronological sequence, but instead derives from a cyclical conception of black American history upon which practically every American black novel and short story has been based. The organization of this book, therefore, is not chronological. Each chapter tries to focus on different aspects of and patterns in that basic cyclical conception.

Chapter One identifies three main cyclical patterns in black fiction as shown in three different novels. Chapter

Two analyzes four works of fiction in order to illustrate various attempts at breaking the cyclical patterns in which black characters find themselves. The third chapter is a study of humor in black fiction as it both evades and intensifies the cyclical patterns in the literature. Chapter Four examines four novels about white America in order to suggest how the cyclical conception unifying black fiction has been created and sustained. The fifth and final chapter is about the nature of heroism and tragedy in black fiction, the ultimate effect of functioning within cyclical patterns on three major heroes.

Not all of the works discussed here are equal in merit. In avoiding comparative or even absolute judgments, however, I have not meant to imply that the question of merit is irrelevant to the subject. My hope in offering a theory of black fiction is to provide a scheme in which judgments of value may continue to be made, perhaps with a stronger sense of the context and unity of the whole. Every one of these works has been born of the same central question: How do black people live in this country? From Paul Laurence Dunbar to Ernest Gaines black authors have pursued either answers to this question or new ways to put it. I suggest that for each of them, regardless of literary movement, of differences in background, viewpoints, locations, styles, capacities of imagination, and degrees of technical ability, the end product has consisted of the same symbols, the same problems, and, indeed, the same conclusions.

I

Lord of the Rings

Toward the end of his autobiography, *Black Boy*, Richard Wright recounts an incident which occurred when, as a young man in Memphis, he had a job grinding lenses in an eyeglass factory. His supervisor interrupted his work one morning to tell him that Harrison, another black worker employed by a rival optical company across the street, held a grudge against Wright. The supervisor said that Harrison carried a knife. Wright and Harrison met that noon after some preliminary stalking, each trying to discover why the other wanted to kill him. When they determined that both of their white supervisors had fabricated the grudge in order to pit them against each other, they agreed to keep quiet and let the joke die.

But the white supervisors persisted. Morning after morning they would approach Wright and Harrison, trying to goad them into fighting. They armed the two of them with knives, and told each to attack without warning. When their strategy failed, the supervisors and a group of other white men asked Wright directly if he would settle his nonexistent grudge with Harrison in a boxing match, for five dollars apiece. Wright refused at first, but Harrison persuaded him that the five dollars would be easy money, that all they would need to do is to pretend to fight and pull punches. The match was announced, to the delight of all the local white men, who offered to buy meals for the combatants. It took place on a Saturday afternoon in a nearby basement before an all-white audience. Wright and Harrison jabbed lightly at the start, then gradually harder. The white men shouted obscenities and cheered wildly. Rounds lasted many minutes. At the end, the two boys had to be pulled apart, having beaten each other senseless.

The point of this autobiographical fragment is made in black fiction regularly. For a black character to be acceptable within a white framework, ordinarily the only framework available to him, he must to a certain extent be brutalized. To become respectable within that framework is to become subhuman, and if one is judged to be subhuman, it follows that his capabilities and aspirations will be treated as subhuman as well. Should the character be brutalized without protest, he satisfies his prescription automatically. Should he attempt to deny or break out of his category, there is resistance on the part of the categorizers, and usually the man becomes violent. If he becomes violent enough, he is considered to be brutal, and is responded to accordingly. In either case he completes a circular definition of someone else's manufacture. Not only does he lead a life of predetermined consequences, but he leads that life by progressing backward.

Wright and Harrison would not speak to each other after their fight because they were both filled with shame. They had punished themselves in the ring for getting in the ring, and they would punish each other afterward as well. Yet there was no objective reason for the shame to be theirs. Starting with a false and illogical act they had been led, coaxed, or pushed into a circumstance where that act became reasonable and true. When the fight was over, Wright and Harrison did hold a grudge against each other, just as their supervisors had originally contended. The madness in the situation did not exist primarily in the hysteria of the crowd, nor even in the confusion of victory and defeat, or of power and impotency, on the parts of the fighters. It existed in the fact that a lie became the truth, and that two people who thought they had known what the truth was wound up living the lie.

It is this element of reversal of reason which extends to every aspect of black fiction, to problems of character and theme as well as to more specific considerations of imagery, heroism, the various relationships among people, religion, and the senses of time and place. Franz Fanon (*Black Skin, White Masks*) observed that the black man in a white society, once taught to conceive of himself physically as an image of the negative, begins to see his whole life as a series of oppositions. This actual process is repeated often in black fiction, particularly in novels that deal with growing up, such as *The Autobiography of an Ex-Colored Man*, *Go Tell It on the Mountain*, and *Their Eyes Were Watching God*, where a child's initiation into a dangerous world begins with his or her acknowledgment of color, difference, in the mirror. In a sense the entire literature is itself a mirror into which the characters are locked. Everything they think, feel, and do seems turned the wrong way, and even when it is not, there are those available to say that it is, and who are able to prove it. Characters in black fiction behave savagely in order to be considered civilized, rise in order to fall, sin in order to gain salvation, are rewarded for virtue by damnation, assert their presence by disappearing, are old when they are young, act as children in old age, are emancipated so that they may be enslaved, see when they are blind, hate in order to love, die in order to live, refuse education in order to learn, and murder in order to create. For every manifestation of inversion and reversal which occurs, however, there is also the awareness of how their lives, given the proper circumstances, ought to look turned around and right side up. The contest which results, between the desire to function within a sane and sensible set of standards and the impossibility of achieving it, is the basic contest of the literature. It ends either in a hero's defeat or in stalemate, and, as in Wright versus Harrison, or Wright and Harrison versus the white citizens, is conceived in a cyclical nightmare.

Native Son

The novel which illustrates the cyclical quality of black fiction most dramatically is *Native Son*. The novel is treacherous because it is readily understandable, yet the fact that it is readily understandable, that all its meanings are on the surface, enlarges its power to terrify. The story seems to explain itself as a social document: Bigger Thomas, nineteen or twenty, black, full of unarticulated hate, is hired as a chauffeur by the rich, white Daltons. The Daltons' daughter, Mary, asks Bigger to drive her to a rendezvous with her forbidden boy friend, a young Communist named Jan Erlone. During the course of the evening, Jan and Mary proceed to overwhelm and confuse Bigger with self-congratulatory gestures which proclaim

Bigger's racial equality. When the party breaks up, Mary is drunk, and Bigger must carry her to her room. The blind Mrs. Dalton enters to see if Mary has returned. Bigger, terrified that he will be discovered and falsely accused, pushes a pillow down over the girl's face in order to keep her quiet. Doing so, he smothers her, panics, and in desperation to hide the crime, shoves Mary's body, beheaded, into the furnace. Trying to protect himself, he makes a blundering attempt to cast suspicion on Jan by suggesting that the Communists have kidnapped Mary. He enlists the help of his girl, Bessie, but afraid that she will give him away, he murders her. Bigger is hunted, captured, tried, defended on social grounds, and left to await execution.

The plot of the novel may be horrifying, but its horror is easily dissipated. Once the sociological explanations of Bigger's behavior have been made, neatly and at length, as they are by his lawyer, Max, that particular level of nightmare, which is the level of action, disappears because the reader feels free of the book's external events as soon as those events have been cleared up by science. When *Native Son* first appeared, its critical acclaim was based on the discovery of its social abstractions. It was considered to be a great and powerful book because it dramatically exposed a series of great and powerful injustices. Only Baldwin differed from most of the critics when he said that *Native Son* was not about injustice, but about the human heart, thereby substituting one abstraction for another.

Native Son is neither about injustice nor the human heart, but about the individual, Bigger Thomas. The novel pivots on a simple exclamation repeated on two occasions by Bigger's mother: "Boy, sometimes I wonder what makes you act like you do" (11, 97). No one in the book gets at the answer to that problem because Bigger lives apart from other people. The outer world, as his author puts it, is "not his world." Bigger's world consists of images, surrealistic distortions of ideas and feelings which grow out of a mind attuned solely to sensations. He is a distortion himself: an upside down man who, when he tries to stand right side up, turns inside out.

His life began backward with a geographical inversion. His family traveled north in the "great migration" expecting to realize emancipation, and received instead a different form of enclosure. They escaped out of one house of bondage into a smaller and more cramped house where the story begins. The Thomases moved north to be able to earn a living and began a slow death of mind and body. They moved up to go down. They emigrated to a colder climate where the heat was stifling. Specifically, they undertook a pilgrimage to the promised land of Chicago which turned out to be hell, despite its Loop, its fake ring of paradise. The city was a butcher of hogs, and was known for its fire.

Hell, then, is where *Native Son* is located. The shame which its characters experience is the shame of the damned. Bigger is told to turn to the wall while his sister dresses and undresses because Vera wants to hide her nakedness from him. Bigger does not like people staring at him either, fearing exposure of secret and nameless sins. His home is the hell of *No Exit*:

> He looked round the room, seeing it for the first time.
> There was no rug on the floor and the plastering on
> the walls and ceiling hung loose in many places.
> There were two worn iron beds, four chairs, an old
> dresser, and a drop-leaf table on which they ate. This
> was much different from Dalton's home. Here all slept
> in one room; there he would have a room for himself
> alone. He smelt food cooking and remembered that
> one could not smell food cooking in Dalton's home;
> pots could not be heard rattling all over the house.
> Each person lived in one room and had a little world
> of his own. He hated this room and all the people
> in it, including himself. (100)

Bigger wants to become an aviator and join the air force, but he cannot fly. He exclaims, "What in hell can a man do?" (24), meaning what can a man do in hell. His friend Gus says, "God'll let you fly when he gives you your wings up in heaven" (20), but Bigger is not going to get to heaven. He has his "flight" (the title of the second section of the novel), but it only goes from one zone of hell to another. He uses the word "hell" continuously, especially in the presence of Bessie, who shares his hell and has a quieter one all to herself. Mary makes him conscious of his blackness; he thinks, "Goddam her soul to hell" (67), which, in a way, he does by placing her body in flames, but he also suffers hell on her account:

> Why was Mary standing there so eagerly, with shining eyes? What could they get out of this? Maybe they did not despise him? But they made him feel his black skin by just standing there looking at him, one holding his hand and the other smiling. He felt he had no physical existence at all right then; he was something he hated, the badge of shame which he knew was attached to a black skin. It was a shadowy region, a No Man's Land. (67)

And there is Chicago all around, the wider hell from which, like his home, there is no exit: "he could not leave Chicago; all roads were blocked" (230).

As a boarder in hell, Bigger is always close to fire and incendiary material. He is condemned by the State as an "infernal monster." The message he reads from the sky-writing plane is "Use Speed Gasoline," potentially useful advice for his burning of Mary. There is a variety of fires inside him: "Bigger laughed, softly at first, then harder, louder, hysterically; feeling something like hot water bubbling inside of him and trying to come out" (39). Whenever he thinks of white folks, "It's like fire" (24), or "like somebody's poking a red hot iron down my throat" (23). One of his duties in the Dalton home is to tend the furnace and keep the coals glowing. As long as the fire rages Bigger is safe. When the flames die down, Mary's bones and his crime are discovered. At one point Mary says to him, "Got a match? Strike it" (64). During his capture Bigger is shot with a fire hose. "Many times, when alone after Max had left him, he wondered wistfully if there was not a set of words which he had in common with others, words which would evoke in others a sense of the same fire that smouldered in him" (337). A mob burns a cross for Bigger. Bigger is sentenced to "burn" in the electric chair.

In the context of hell, furnaces become the centers of activity. There is the actual furnace that holds Mary's body, and there are the figurative furnaces of Bigger's rage and of the home in which he is forced to live. In order to fit Mary in the furnace Bigger must cut off her head. In order for Bigger, his family and friends, to fit into the furnaces of their own tenements, their heads also had to roll. Mary's decapitation is only the physical counterpart of a neater, more sophisticated and bloodless execution: the action by which a man's head (his intelligence, his source of feeling, aspiration, achievement) is removed so that he may more easily be closeted, categorized, buried, or cremated. Dan McCall (*The Example of Richard Wright*) points out that as an act of symbolic revenge it is only natural that Bigger must always go for the head—for the rat's head at the outset of the novel; for Mary's head; for Bessie's head; for the head of the vigilante hunting him on the roof; even metaphorically for the head of his mother: "Well, don't bite her head off, Vera said" (14). The images of his spiritual decapitation and Mary's real one fuse in a dream:

> Out of the surrounding silence and darkness came
> the quiet ringing of a distant church bell, thin, faint,
> but clear. It tolled, soft, then loud, then still louder,
> so loud that he wondered where it was. It sounded
> suddenly directly above his head and when he looked
> it was not there but went on tolling and with each
> passing moment he felt an urgent need to run and hide
> as though the bell were sounding a warning and he
> stood on a street corner in a red glare of light like that
> which came from the furnace and he had a big package

in his arms so wet and slippery and heavy that he could
scarcely hold onto it and he wanted to know what was
in the package and he stopped near an alley corner
and unwrapped it and the paper fell away and he
saw—it was his own head... (156)

The substitution of his head for Mary's is made not only
because Bigger had had his "head" removed long before he
had actually decapitated Mary, but because by tormenting
Bigger with futile and anachronistic gestures of good will,
Mary only served to remind Bigger that he had no head
with which to receive or apprehend her gestures. To Bigger
all such gestures were but dimly perceivable; therefore, his
responses to them were mumbles. After centuries of historical decapitation, Mary was saying "think and feel" to
a man who had lost his ability to do so.

What does it mean to lose one's head? We are traveling
through a hell called heaven, through a labyrinthine kind
of madhouse where, in one way or another, everyone has
lost his head. There is a great deal of hysteria in the novel:
hysteria in a poolroom brawl where Bigger, afraid to go
ahead with a robbery of his own design, transfers his fears
to his friend Gus and starts a fracas in order to abort the
plot; hysteria in Bigger's cell; in the outcries of Bessie and
his mother. It is also a feature of this madhouse that everybody in it accuses everybody else of being crazy. Mary's
mouthings sound "crazy" to Bigger. Gus, G.H., and Vera
all call Bigger crazy. Yet the State's prosecutor, Buckley,
will not accept an insanity plea on Bigger's behalf. According to Buckley's definition of justice, and sanity, only a
sane and rational man could have committed Bigger's
crimes. While depicting the crimes as animalistic and
"monstrous," Buckley nevertheless insists upon Bigger's
sanity, because if Bigger had been judged insane, his punishment would not have been sufficient. Much of Buckley's
effort, therefore, goes into proving the sanity of Bigger's
insane crimes, which effort is a form of madness in itself.
The only bona fide madman in the novel, one who is officially recognized and certified as a lunatic, is the black

intellectual who is thrown into Bigger's cell, who demands his "papers." The irony of his brief appearance is that although he raves and grips the bars of the cell and frightens Bigger and the other prisoners with the outer trappings of lunacy, what he says about having been robbed of life is, in fact, quite reasonable. His madness is identified not by crazy ideas voiced in a sane context, but by the reverse.

In the madhouse people also wear masks. In jail Bigger begins to see Jan "as though someone had performed an operation upon his eyes, or as though someone had snatched a deforming mask from Jan's face" (268). When Bigger has his interview with the Daltons, he sits squirming in the living room, hat in hand, feet shuffling, repeating "sir" and "ma'am." Earlier that afternoon he had torn around the poolroom like a lion, but here in the elegant white home, a Wonderland to him, even his huge size, like Alice's, diminishes, and he assumes the face and features of the "house nigger." He wears the mask, in the sense of Dunbar's poem, as a dual means of self-concealment and self-protection.

According to Henri Bergson's theory of laughter, the mask is a comic instrument, a mechanical object imposed on the suppleness and flexibility of the human face. The force of such impositions is the interruption of human momentum or the human form; thus animals are also funny insofar as their movements and behavior are associated with human beings. But in *Native Son*, despite the fact that characters both wear masks and are identified as animals (Bigger variously as an ape, dog, and gorilla; Vera and Bessie as dogs), no humor is produced. Human momentum is broken all the time in *Native Son* (in a wider sense, the entire story is about the breaking of one man's momentum), yet no comedy occurs because we are merely shown the causal conditions of laughter. Between the perception of the comic situation and the comedy itself lies the context which cuts the laughter off. "It's funny how the white folks treat us, ain't it?" says Bigger. " 'It better be funny,' Gus said" (20).

There is no laughter in the madhouse, but there are

games. Bigger and Gus play make-believe, one acting out the part of an army general, the other of J. P. Morgan. They simulate a military-industrial complex, and play roles of enormous prestige and power. Yet the joy in their game is also its pathos. Like participants in a minstrel show, they derive their fun from taking on parts which they, as actors and audience both, know can never be realized. Their language can be exaggerated, they can play their parts to the hilt, and they can engage in satire and fantasy simultaneously, because the very freedom of their game is created and encouraged by an external constriction, the fact that their real aspirations will always be relegated to the world of game-playing. Gus will take orders from Bigger in the charade, but not when it comes to robbing Blum's store, not in real life. In real life Bigger is not to be trusted.

The question is, where is Bigger's real life, and how is it to be distinguished from the varieties of unreality in which he lives? Bigger enjoys the world of the movies, not only the movies themselves, but the movie houses as well, which provide the atmosphere of kings in royal boxes (the theater he goes to is called The Regal) and the darkness that makes Bigger inconspicuous. Yet even the movie (dream) house is not safe from Buckley. At the trial Buckley reveals not only that Bigger went to the movies on the day of the murder, but that he sneaked in without paying. Nor is it only Buckley who invades the movie world, but reality as well. One of the films Bigger watches is about Communists and millionaires. The second is *Trader Horn*, about Africa, but Bigger only wants to think about the story of the "smart people," *The Gay Woman*. Gus tells him that "rich, white women'll go to bed with anybody, from a poodle on up. Shucks, they even have their chauffeurs" (53). Bigger daydreams:

> Yes, his going to work for the Daltons was something big. Maybe Mr. Dalton was a millionaire. Maybe he had a daughter who was a hot kind of girl; maybe she spent lots of money; maybe she'd like to come to the south side and see the sights sometimes. Or maybe

she had a secret sweetheart and only he would know
about it because he would have to drive her around;
maybe she would give him money not to tell. (36)

The terrible aspect of this conjecture, of course, is that it
all, or most of it, comes true. The satisfaction of the day-
dream perverts the dream into a nightmare. When the
movies are over, Gus remarks, "Swell, wasn't it?" Bigger
answers, "Yeah. It was a killer" (37).

In the madhouse people do not wish to be looked at,
and yet in one way or another everyone is blind, so the
fear of exposure is groundless. In all cases but Mrs. Dalton's,
blindness is psychosomatic, but like the others, Mrs. Dalton
has a spiritual handicap as well as a physical one. A latter-
day Grandissime, she and her husband, as Max points out,
cannot see the malevolent condition which they serve and
perpetuate. Similarly, Mary and Jan cannot see the empti-
ness of their charity. Bessie is blinded by tears and fright.
At different times Bigger is blinded by snow, light, and
rage. In the presence of Jan and Max he feels "transparent,"
invisible (68). At the end of the novel Max "groped for his
hat like a blind man" (392). The two abstract conceptions
which inform *Native Son*, love and justice, are also traditionally blind.

Only one person, Bigger, gains a kind of sight in the
novel, but the vision which Bigger gains is also distorted.
It is made up of the images that appear when one holds a
magnifying glass close to the face, and then moves it further and further away from one's eyes until the picture
reflected in the glass comes in at once clearly and upside
down. Bigger begins the story seeing everything in a haze.
The sight which he eventually achieves is in sharp focus,
but out of whack:

> He felt in the quiet presence of his brother, mother,
> and sister a force, inarticulate and unconscious,
> making for living without thinking, making for peace
> and habit, making for a hope that blinded. He felt
> that they wanted and yearned to see life in a certain
> way; they needed a certain picture of the world; there

was one way of living they preferred above all others; and they were blind to what did not fit. They did not want to see what others were doing if that doing did not feed their own desires. All one had to do was be bold, do something nobody thought of. The whole thing came to him in the form of a powerful and simple feeling; there was in everyone a great hunger to believe that made him blind, and if he could see while others were blind, then he could get what he wanted and never be caught at it. Now, who on earth would think that he, a black timid Negro boy, would murder and burn a rich white girl and would sit and wait for his breakfast like this? Elation filled him. (102)

It is perfectly apt for Bigger to watch Jan and Mary, as he does, through a rearview mirror, because the final understanding which he reaches of Jan and of Mary, of the Daltons, Max, of the entire white world and his relation to it, is completely turned around: "What I killed for must've been good" (392).

Everything is turned around in this way in *Native Son*, even the idea of color. Here darkness, customarily connected with evil, dishonor, or ignorance, offers safety, whereas whiteness is a source of terror. In black fiction generally, white is the color of suffocation, disorientation, deafness, blindness, of threat, of being cornered. It is also the non-color by which all others, including black, may be swallowed up. In *Beetlecreek*, William Demby cites "the shriveled paleness" of Trapp's soul. In *dem*, William Kelley's Harlem girls chant about a polar bear coming to enslave them. The domineering chef in Claude McKay's *Home to Harlem* prizes the whiteness of his uniform, as does Mr. Watford, the man without feeling, in Paule Marshall's "Barbados" (*Soul Clap Hands and Sing*). Glory, the shrew of Ann Petry's *Country Place*, is described solely by the blondness of her hair. John Grimes (*Go Tell It on the Mountain*) "knew that time was indifferent, like snow and ice" (268). In Wright, white signifies nothingness: "to Bigger and his kind white people were not really people; they were a sort of great natural force, like a stormy sky looming overhead"(109).

Whiteness and fear have, of course, been connected before. Melville explored and theorized about the monumental supernaturalism of the albino whale; Coleridge's nightmare Life-in-Death was "white as leprosy"; Death itself rode a pale horse; and nothing in poetry so conveys the awful sense of blankness as Wallace Stevens' "Snow Man." But there is a difference in such perceptions in black and white literature. In the examples above, and more could be cited, whiteness usually is terrifying only when it is attached to objects already terrible in themselves; whereas in black fiction the fearfulness of white is the rule, not the exception, and is wholly independent of customarily frightening objects. The only instances in which the fearful qualities of the color and the object are cooperative are those where the object concerned happens to be a man (or as in Ellison's "Flying Home," a man wearing a sheet). Among white authors one rarely finds a character to be terrifying, as Bigger finds Mr. Dalton, simply because he is white.

Time, too, is out of joint here, as it is in most of black fiction. Characters such as Constance of Countee Cullen's *One Way to Heaven* and Jake of McKay's *Home to Harlem* cling tenaciously to the present not out of simple hedonism, but because the past and future have no meaning for them. Neither does the act of telling time. *If He Hollers Let Him Go* and *Native Son* both begin with the noise of clocks, but the clocks serve only as instruments of alarm. At the conclusion of his story, Ellison's Invisible Man resolves to live underground, observing that "the end was in the beginning" (494). In his introduction to *Black Thunder*, Arna Bontemps declares, "Time is not a river. Time is a pendulum." Toomer says in "Carma" (*Cane*), "Time and space have no meaning in a canefield" (19).

Wright dealt with this question before *Native Son*, in "Long Black Song," of *Uncle Tom's Children*. In that story

Sarah's baby is given a clock without hands as a toy. "But why let her tear your clock up?" asks the white drummer who is about to seduce her.

> "It ain no good."
> "You could have it fixed."
> "We ain got no money t be fixin' no clocks."
> "Haven't you got a clock?"
> "Naw."
> "But how do you keep time?"
> "We git erlong widout time."
> "But how do you know when to get up in the morning?"
> "We just git up, thas all."
> "But how do you know what time it is when you get up?"
> "We git up wid the sun."
> "And at night, how do you tell when it's night?"
> "It gits dark when the sun goes down."
> "Haven't you ever had a clock?"
> She laughed and turned her face toward the silent fields. (178)

The point is that time is only useful when one's life is changed during or by it. When no change occurs, it merely becomes a measurement of stasis, as it is for Sarah. To have clocks and watches around is, in fact, worse than not owning such instruments, because they only serve as reminders of a world in which time does have meaning. This comments obliquely on a world in which a linear conception of history has meaning, a world different from the one Wright is depicting.

Time is out of joint in *Native Son* because a madhouse has no need for time, or accurate time. Bigger has a way of continually forgetting the time. As soon as he earns enough money the first thing he plans to buy is a gold watch that will be completely useless to him. Mr. Dalton begins most of his sentences with "Now" when he usually means "Never." Peggy, the Daltons' cook, wants the household to run like a clock, but Bigger's crime upsets her schedules.

When the correct time is known, trouble usually follows. The alarm clock that opens the book signals the entrance of a rat. The timing is off for the robbery of Blum's. In Mary's room the clock with the glowing dial serves as a witness to murder. Bigger's alibi depends on a knowledge of time. When Bigger confesses to Buckley it is observed that "he came through like a clock" (287).

The maddest aspect of the madhouse is the particular crime of which Bigger is accused. It is not murder after all, but rape. Murder, in all other situations, would be the most heinous crime imaginable, especially a brutal murder involving the hacking up of a pretty girl; yet initially the coroner's inquest is desperate to prove, and the State chooses to find, Bigger guilty of Mary's rape ("the central crime is rape" [377]), thereby placing rape above murder in an upside down hierarchy. In a mad context, however, that ranking makes sense, because murder only represents the destruction of white by black, a terminal concern, whereas rape metaphorically represents the assertion of Bigger's black manhood in a white world. The State declares that it is this assertion, as an idea, which is intolerable, and must be punished as the capital offense. Moreover, it must be punished by death because death alone can cancel out the sexual phantasmagoria regarding blacks which the white characters have created out of their wretched imaginations. (At one point even the wretched imaginations get out of hand: "Your Honor, must not this infernal monster have burned her body to destroy evidence of offenses worse than rape?" [376].) The white guilt here is enormous, and the main objective of the State is to generate enough hate to neutralize that guilt.

Bigger does not rape Mary, but he might have, at least in terms of the spirit. Mary teased Bigger with her body in the car and as he carried her upstairs, but throughout the evening she had also teased him with her mind: "Why was Mary standing there so eagerly, with shining eyes?" (67). She had said to Bigger, look at me, my big house, my free and extravagant life, and you can have everything you want. Bigger was aroused, in sexual terms, to manhood:

It seemed that her actions had evoked fear and shame in him. But when he thought hard about it it seemed impossible that they could have. He really did not know just where that fear and shame had come from; it had just been there, that was all. Each time he had come in contact with her it had risen hot and hard. (108)

The sexual terms recur when Bigger begins to experience a number of different passions: "He hated Britten [Dalton's detective] so hot and hard, while standing there with sleepy eyes and parted lips, that he would gladly have grabbed the iron shovel from the corner and split his skull in two" (153). Before the murder, Bigger had been tense; afterward "he felt a lessening of tension in his muscles" (109). And Bessie tells him that they will accuse him of rape:

Had he raped her? Yes, he had raped her. Every time he felt as he had felt that night he raped. But rape was not what one did to women. Rape was what one felt when one's back was against a wall and one had to strike out, whether one wanted to or not to keep the pack from killing one. He committed rape every time he looked into a white face. He was a long, taut piece of rubber which a thousand white hands had stretched to the snapping point, and when he snapped it was rape. But it was rape when he cried out in hate deep in his heart as he felt the strain of living day by day. That, too, was rape. (213–214)

Buckley was right about rape all along, not in fact, but in what he guessed and dimly comprehended: that Bigger had indeed been on the verge of rape that night, on the verge of becoming aware that he had human possibilities. If he had been permitted to live after having committed a crime like that, the State's guilt would have been unbearable.

There can be no guilt in the madhouse, nor can there be any love. Bessie is Bigger's girl, but Bigger, as he readily admits to Max, does not love Bessie. He does not love her, first, because she is, according to an inverted criterion, unlovely. The women who are designated as beautiful in the book are Jean Harlow, Ginger Rogers, and Janet Gaynor, the pin-ups decorating the wall of Bigger's room in the Dalton house, photographs left there by a black man named Green, Bigger's predecessor. Bessie is not called beautiful; she is merely property. We only learn that she has a family name, Mears, after she is dead. She is owned by the people for whom she cleans house, by the booze that sustains and dulls her, and by Bigger (" 'You got a girl, Bigger?' Mary asked. 'I got a girl,' he said" [75]), who uses her in bed and, like Corley in Joyce's "Two Gallants," for petty theft. Bessie is a usable commodity not only to the end, but afterward. Even in death her body is essential as evidence.

Bigger is accused of having committed "two of the most horrible crimes in the history of American civilization" (346). The representation of American civilization suits the madhouse well. Wright's definition of civilization is like Thurber's: the wolves eat the rabbits in order to civilize them. Here the civilized include Britten, Buckley, the Daltons and the mob; while the uncivilized, the animals, are the Thomases, Gus, G.H., and Bessie who, partly for their own good, must be hidden away or destroyed. Chief among the civilized are Mr. and Mrs. Dalton, who because of their wealth, position, and especially their professional philanthropy, symbolize the height which a democratic civilization can reach. They pose for the news photographers like the couple in Grant Wood's *American Gothic* and are honored for the American dream which they are and have made.

Yet Bigger, too, has forged an American dream and like McTeague, with whom he has much in common, has done so at great pains, and with much self-sacrifice. In his own version of the American way, he has plotted and saved and pulled himself up by his own bootstraps. The facts that his particular American dream had to be realized in his own dark and separate America, that his America is upside down, and that his dream is a recurrent nightmare do not detract from or lessen the truth that by the end of the novel Bigger has indeed created something very big. In a madhouse as on a frontier, all things are possible. Even murder, says Max, can be an act of creation. If that is so, Bigger the murderer becomes the god of creation. He has created not only an American dream, but his own divinity as well.

Of the twelve Apostles the most mysterious was Thomas. He was devoted to Jesus ("let us also go, that we may die with him," John 11:16), but he was a shadowy, despondent man who believed without joy or hope, and tended toward gloom. He also only trusted in what he could see with his own eyes, and was curiously absent at the resurrection (John 21:19–24). Bigger Thomas is also a dark figure who only believes in what he sees. He too develops a great devotion, but not to another man. Bigger becomes an apostle of himself. The only resurrection he would attend would be his own.

As befits a savior, prophecies attend him on all sides. The political poster on the signboard near his home shows Buckley, running for State's attorney, pointing his finger directly at Bigger: "If You Break The Law, You Can't Win" (16). Near the end Bigger tells Max, "I knew that some time or other they was going to get me for something. I'm black. I don't have to do nothing for 'em to get me. The first white finger they point at me, I'm a goner, see?" (325). Peggy tells Bigger that his most troublesome task in the Dalton household will be taking out the ashes (59). The device Wright uses (here and in *Uncle Tom's Children* as well) of describing human actions in terms of the motions of disconnected parts of the body foreshadows Mary's burial. "Stop prophesying about me" (13), Bigger warns his mother, but the prophecies persist, nevertheless. What Bigger will do, what will happen to Bigger, and what Bigger will become are questions on which every life in the novel depends.

It is Max who first hits upon the notion that Bigger's killing of Mary was an act of creation, by which he means that Bigger, who was predetermined to do nothing all his life, had found in the act of murder a way to do something. But Bigger creates more than murder when he smothers Mary. Like Joe Christmas of *Light in August*, he creates himself. There was no rape; Bigger was born of an immaculate conception. In an upside-down world murder becomes a sacred ceremony, and even though this particular nativity was attended by no star shining in the East (the sky was full of snow that night), Bigger himself senses the hallowed quality of the scene. Before decapitating Mary, he pauses "in an attitude of prayer" (91), because he senses that by this act he has accomplished a miracle. He becomes the Father who creates the Son in himself.

Here, then, is the native Son who would make the blind (Mrs. Dalton) to see, the lame (Gus) to walk again, who would purify and cleanse the wicked and ignorant (Bessie), and who would lead the little children (Buddy). Yet Mrs. Dalton clings to her blindness, physical and spiritual; Gus is kicked to the floor of the poolroom; the cures Bigger brings Bessie are corruption and death; and at one point he even considers murdering Buddy for fear of betrayal. It is all backward, because Bigger as Jesus is backward. He, too, has his last supper, of bread, but he eats alone. He has not one Judas, but many. All of his disciples would readily betray him. They spread the word, but only of his guilt. Shortly after his birth—the murder—instead of receiving gifts from the three wise men, G.H., Gus, and Doc, Bigger brings gifts, stolen gifts, to them. Unlike his forebear, he resists fiercely on the roof, his mount, and though he is not crucified literally, he is held to await a crucifixion more up to date: "Two men stretched his arms out, as though about to crucify him; they placed a foot on each of his wrists, making them sink deep down in the snow. His eyes closed, slowly, and he was swallowed in darkness" (253).

Bigger is the God of the Old Testament as well as the New. Surrounded by false gods such as the white man's Jesus, he rips what is to him a fake ikon, the cross, from his throat and casts it away. Jan and Mary sing "Swing Low, Sweet Chariot," a slavery song of escape, to him, but Bigger knows that that chariot cannot swing so low as to pick him up and carry him home (77). He is an all-powerful and vengeful god of a special creation. In his cell, the Reverend Mr. Hammond reminds him of the wonder of Genesis, but that story has no meaning for Bigger. Bigger has had his own genesis, no less wonderful to him than the story of the

Bible. "And God saw every thing that he had made, and, behold, it was very good" (Genesis 2:31). "What I killed for must've been good," Bigger declares. "It must have been good" (392).

This final observation of Bigger's is the ultimate inversion. It is the proclamation of a man who has discovered the full meaning of the kingdom of hell. "I myself am hell," said Milton's Satan. Bigger, too, is hell, a hell within the maze of hells around him. His birth in murder was not a second coming but merely one in a thousand such comings, and one, Wright suggests, if nothing changes, which may promise thousands more. If, as Buckley declared, the law is holy, then in the same awful sense of that word Bigger is holy, and so is his ghost. The court clerk asks, "Bigger Thomas will you rise?" The question is rhetorical.

Go Tell It on the Mountain

The cyclical damnation which Baldwin depicts in *Go Tell It on the Mountain* is less sensational and picturesque than Wright's, and less mythological, although its language is more heightened and it draws more heavily on Christian doctrine. That the novel should have been a product of what Robert Lowell termed the "tranquilized fifties" is remarkable, because in certain ways *Go Tell It on the Mountain* imitates its era. There is an external and formal tidiness to this book which belies a monstrous internal chaos, a chaos made up, not as in *Native Son*, primarily of action, but of ideas, feelings, spiritual messages and intuitions which hound and confuse the characters. We are shown a half dozen people mountain-climbing under the sight and power of a colossal god who straddles both testaments. We watch them strive toward that god, as God the Father, and at the same time see the god grow larger, more terrible, and further out of reach.

Baldwin's story is of fathers and sons, specifically of Gabriel and John Grimes, and there are two sides to the story. The account of Gabriel's life begins with his waiting to see whether or not a local mob of white men will burn down his house. Gabriel is "the apple of his mother's eye" (89). He grows up wildly, earning the hatred and envy of his sister, Florence. When Florence turns twenty-six, and can take neither Gabriel nor their home any longer, she moves north, delivering the care of their God-ridden mother into Gabriel's hands. Now Gabriel is forced to reform. His mother "lay waiting . . . for his surrender to the Lord" (119). The surrender comes in a miraculously quick conversion when Gabriel receives a sign in the form of a tree to lean on: "this was the beginning of his life as a man" (125). He becomes a preacher, and a year after the death of his mother, he marries Deborah, the holy lady and pariah of the town who, at the age of sixteen, had been dragged into the fields and raped by the same white men who years earlier had threatened to burn down Gabriel's house.

Equipped with a resonant voice and a talent for sermons, Gabriel becomes renowned as a preacher, yet he remains open to temptation. He meets a serving girl, Esther, and he falls. Esther bears him a son named Royal, whom Gabriel disowns and whose existence Gabriel denies. In fear of having his sin discovered, he sends Esther away to die. Later, Royal gets "hisself killed in Chicago" (197). Deborah learns the truth, but does not reveal it, even when dying. As did Florence before him, Gabriel comes north to New York, meets and marries Elizabeth, who already has one son, John, and who bears Gabriel another, whom once again Gabriel calls Royal. The novel opens as this second Royal is stabbed in a street fight. Gabriel, Elizabeth, Florence, and John go to church in order to pray for Royal's moral improvement. That night in church Gabriel sees John receive the Word which had remained unavailable to himself.

Everything in Gabriel's life is a contradiction. His life is hell because the elements of each contradiction are at war inside him. His name, Gabriel Grimes, is a contradiction of terms: the angel of filth. The name Gabriel means "man of god," and that, too, is a contradiction, as Gabriel is not a man of God in any sense but the professional. He can appear to be different sizes and shapes simultaneously: at once the pettiest figure in the novel, and the one who

Lord of the Rings   37

dominates everyone around him. He possesses both the smallest and largest conscience, the longest and shortest memory, the highest and lowest sense of righteousness. Opposing forces flourish in him, as they do in Florence, who in the act of love-making "burned with longing and froze with rage" (111), whose "tears came down like burning rain" (117). At an advanced age Gabriel is baptized in water, and becomes preacher to the Temple of the Fire Baptized.

What he wants is redemption through repentance, because he believes that for him redemption will mean that all the irreconcilables will be resolved. He develops an elaborate system of holy living whereby he can impose simplistic penalties upon himself. The penalties are imposed whenever Gabriel has sinned, that is, behaved honestly according to his own passionate nature. Consistent with his inconsistencies, he creates lies to confront and correct his truth. At heart, he is like Gatsby without stamina, wishing to be reborn after every transgression, seeking deliverance, in the sense of birth, from his own frail mind.

Yet at the same time he longs to perpetuate himself. Each son born to him is named Royal because Gabriel wants to create a lineage of kings. In terms of his own simple-minded mythologizing, it ought to have been glorious to have had a son named Royal by Esther, who was named for a queen, but the union was unholy, and Gabriel had to seek another heir. John can provide no lineage for Gabriel because John, who was born out of wedlock to Richard and Elizabeth, is not his natural son. The second Royal is his natural son, but the son turns upon the father, calling him a "black bastard." Bastards are denied the kingdom of heaven: "A bastard shall not enter into the congregation of the Lord; even to their tenth generation shall they not enter into the congregation of the Lord" (Deuteronomy 23:2). John is technically a bastard, yet John's salvation is the great hope of the novel.

How can John the bastard be expected to achieve heaven, and how can heaven be denied to Gabriel, the angel of the Lord? The contradictions keep accumulating. The Gabriel of the Bible is God's herald who brings great news: "Fear not, Zacharias: for thy prayer is heard; and thy wife Elisabeth shall bear thee a son, and thou shalt call his name John. And thou shalt have joy and gladness; and many shall rejoice at his birth. For he shall be great in the sight of the Lord, and shall drink neither wine nor strong drink; and he shall be filled with the Holy Ghost, even from his mother's womb. And many of the children of Israel shall he turn to the Lord their God" (Luke 1:13–16). John Grimes brings no joy or gladness to Gabriel or anyone else. He is a gloomy, sullen child, called "frog eyes" (reminiscent of a plague), at whose illegitimate birth no one rejoiced. The ghost that fills him is the terror of Gabriel, and as for turning others to the Lord, it is his own conversion which is the center of his and everyone else's attention.

To Zacharias and Elisabeth was born John, who became John the Baptist:

> I indeed baptize you with water unto repentance:
> but he that cometh after me is mightier than I, whose
> shoes I am not worthy to bear: he shall baptize you
> with the Holy Ghost, and with fire. Whose fan is in
> his hand, and he will thoroughly purge his floor, and
> gather his wheat into the garner; but he will burn up
> the chaff with unquenchable fire. Then cometh Jesus
> from Galilee to Jordan unto John, to be baptized of
> him. But John forbade him, saying, I have no need to be
> baptized of thee, and comest thou to me? And Jesus
> answering said unto him, Suffer it to be so now: for thus
> it becometh us to fulfill all righteousness. And Jesus,
> when he was baptized, went up straightway out of the
> water: and, lo, the heavens were opened unto him,
> and he saw the Spirit of God descending like a dove,
> and lighting upon him.   (Matthew 3:11–17)

John the Baptist was the answer to a prayer against barrenness, but the presence of John Grimes only serves to remind Gabriel of his own spiritual barrenness. Gabriel despises John both because John is a bastard and therefore unclean, and because John's existence, like a bad sign, persistently reminds Gabriel of his own bastard, the one he made and let die. As a young man, Gabriel was dragged kicking and shouting into the holy waters, where he sputtered and was blessed in the name of John, whose namesake he is obliged, by marriage, to love. No heavens opened up to Gabriel on that day, and no Spirit of God descended: "and though at first they thought that it was the power of the Lord that worked in him, they realized as he rose, still kicking, and with his eyes tightly shut, that it was only fury, and too much water in his nose" (93). The water scorched Gabriel, and in turn, he brings a furious, evangelical fire to John, but John feels "no warmth for him from this fire" (265).

Gabriel is supposed to be the emissary from heaven, and yet, like Bigger, he only suffers damnation. He too, was part of the "great migration" north, emigrating from one hell into another for purposes of salvation. He calls Broadway hell because the Great White Way is not the narrow way. But Gabriel is his own hell, no matter where he is located. Like Bigger, too, he was born to be close to fire. White men threaten to burn down his home. Esther "was associated in his mind with flame: with fiery leaves in the autumn, and the fiery sun going down in the evening over the farthest hill, and with the eternal fires of Hell" (152). He continually has dreams of hell, and of Satan, and the hell of which he dreams is always sexual. Inevitably, he manages to substitute a real hell for his dream, creating his own special entrapment: Esther "sat down at the table, smiling, to wait for him. He tried to do everything as quickly as possible, the shuttering of windows, and locking of doors. But his fingers were stiff and slippery: his heart was in his mouth. And it came to him that he was barring every exit to this house, except the exit through the kitchen, where Esther sat" (163–164). In his self-torturing imagination Esther is the she-devil, the queen of hell's kitchen, called appropriately after the biblical queen of revenge. The Book of Esther is noteworthy in the Old Testament for the fact that it contains no mention of God.

Yet God is all over Gabriel, every minute, like the baptismal waters around and through him. Gabriel is not merely climbing a mountain of deliverance; he is climbing that mountain with another mountain of guilt on his back: "this burden was heavier than the heaviest mountain and he carried it in his heart. With each step that he took his burden grew heavier, and his breath became slow and harsh, and, of a sudden, cold sweat stood out on his brow and drenched his back" (118). Elizabeth is also climbing a mountain, in order to reach a simple, peaceful place for her family. Florence's mountain is built up of a lifetime of vengeance against her brother. John's mountain was erected for him and is meant to lead to a state of grace. Everyone is making one sort of climb or another, and at the same time everyone speaks of bringing everyone else "low."

Everybody also speaks of wanting to change, to convert, but in *Go Tell It on the Mountain* there are no changes. Elizabeth carries John, Richard's son, through the streets of Harlem. Richard, a fatherless child, had killed himself after having been falsely accused of being a thief. Now his own fatherless child survives, and Elizabeth thinks "of the boys who had gone to prison. Were they there still? Would John be one of these boys one day? These boys, now, who stood before drugstore windows, before poolrooms, on every street corner, who whistled after her, whose lean bodies fairly rang, it seemed, with idleness, and malice, and frustration" (242). She considers the cycles, not only thinking of John's future, but implicitly of the future of other Elizabeths: Will her baby grow up to become one of those boys whistling at her now? Will he have a son, too, and then die a suicide, leaving his own Elizabeth forever to be whistled at?

Florence wants her Frank to change, to become sophisticated and cultivated—"And what do you want me to do, Florence? You want me to turn white?" (109)—but Frank's only change is to walk out on Florence. Florence would like to be white herself, but the bleaching creams do not work. Esther will not change (convert) for Gabriel; instead she converts Gabriel, not on the threshing floor but the kitchen floor, back to what he really is. Gabriel's whole being is consumed with the idea of change, but Gabriel will never be different from what he is despite all the ghosts and demons he conjures up to placate his ignorance: "You can't change nothing, Gabriel," says Florence, "You ought to know that by now" (58). Nor will God change to suit Gabriel or anyone. To the fatherless people of the novel—and everyone here is fatherless—God is the everlasting father whose will is steadfast and permanent.

Everybody wants to change, because everybody wants to be saved, and salvation here is connected with change. There is supposed to be salvation and safety in the church. Deborah, who was a nurse and prophetess in the Bible, plays the same roles in the novel, in which roles lie both her safety and salvation. Salvation means a kind of deliverance toward the light. John, Gabriel, Elizabeth, Florence, and the other members of the church are all seeking the light. And yet, as Baldwin suggested in the title of one of his essays ("Carmen Jones: The Dark is Light Enough," *Notes of a Native Son*), the light can have its own kind of darkness: "The moment of salvation is a blinding light" (137). Florence wants light as light pertains to color; thus the light she seeks is false. John's effort is to seek the light of God and of self-understanding, both of which are obscure to him. Richard does begin to find a light, but at the end Richard is found in his prison cell, like Samson in Gaza, "his eyes staring upward with no light, dead among the scarlet sheets" (235). Gabriel wants the light of divine vision, but he is blinded by the baptismal waters, which prevent him from seeing himself clearly. In the Book of Daniel, Gabriel brings Daniel a vision, but our Gabriel is only capable of a blind rage, he who is persistently searching for visions and miraculous signs, whose inspired sermon is on Isaiah, the Eagle-Eyed.

Here, as elsewhere in black fiction, light and daylight, as aspects of whiteness, are sources of fear. Throughout much of the literature, light serves not as a benign or inspirational force, but as an instrument of entrapment and exposure, like a search lamp, pinning characters down, revealing their real or imagined guilts, and making, or threatening to make, them vulnerable to their pursuers. "You better gid a move on," Mingo warns Harriet in Langston Hughes's *Not Without Laughter*, "Daylight ain't holdin' itself back for you" (104). In *If He Hollers Let Him Go* Bob Jones keeps his eyes "shut tight against the mornings" (95). Deaths occur in daylight: in *Home to Harlem* Jerco's body is discovered at dawn; in *Go Tell It on the Mountain* the flogged soldier lay "exposed to the cold white air of morning" (190).

Metaphorically, light is also occasionally linked up with a peculiar kind of ignorance. For all the claims for the value of books and learning on the part of Toomer, Hughes, Wright, and others, education in black fiction often carries with it severe penalties of loneliness and isolation. Bob Jones in *If He Hollers Let Him Go*, Emma Lou Morgan in Wallace Thurman's *The Blacker the Berry*, the narrators of Toomer's "Avey" and "Fern" (*Cane*), and of Baldwin's "Sonny's Blues," are all set apart from their people because of their gifts, schooling, and intellectual curiosity. James W. Johnson's Ex-Colored Man deliberately avoids college, and the Invisible Man's disintegration begins at his valedictory address. At certain points, the "enlightenment" of these characters has meant a loss of feeling for roots, a loss of self. As Wright's Big Boy ("Big Boy Leaves Home," *Uncle Tom's Children*) observes, if you're standing in the light, you cannot see into the dark.

In seeking the light, John associates the darkness of his body with the darkness of the soul. He feels an overwhelming guilt attached to both darknesses:

> And he struggled to flee—out of this darkness, out of this company—into the land of the living, so high, so far away. Fear was upon him, a more deadly fear than he had ever known, as he turned and turned in the darkness, as he moaned, and stumbled, and crawled through darkness, finding no hand, no voice, finding no door. *Who are these? Who are they?* They were the despised and rejected, the wretched and the spat upon, the earth's off-scouring; and he was in their company, and they would swallow up his soul. (273)

There is no reason for these feelings to occur to him. The connection of guilt and darkness has assaulted his imagination by way of historical inheritance, not because of any sin which he has committed. John's only identifiable sin in the novel is masturbation. Even though he says that "the darkness of his sin was in the hardheartedness with which he resisted God's power" (15), he eventually gives in to that power. Gabriel, on the other hand, really does possess a darkness of the soul. He is not only the prince of darkness here, but the angel and prophet of darkness as well.

Gabriel is, in the deepest sense of the phrase, a living panic. Moreover, he is an inarticulate panic who uses his fists automatically, and who never seems to be able to find the proper words for an occasion except when preaching. In the pulpits he has all the words, words which in fact are nothing more than words, and have no conceptual relationship to him, nor any bearings on his actions. Yet he has a great need for words, as if some magic in the words themselves can do something for him, can hold him intact. People like Richard and Esther are eternal mysteries to Gabriel because they celebrate their inarticulateness. They are always and naturally themselves, without verbal confirmations. But for Gabriel language affords protection:

> " I done told you before," he said—he had not
> ceased working over the moaning Roy, and was
> preparing new to dab the wound with iodine—"that
> I didn't want you coming in here and using that gutter
> language in front of my children."
> "Don't you worry about my language, brother,"
> she said with spirit, "you better start worrying about
> your *life*. What these children hear ain't going to do
> them near as much harm as what they *see*."   (51)

John is considered to be bright because he does have words. The stone lions posted as sentinels outside the New York Public Library at 42nd Street may serve to keep John from the words and to guard the words from John, but unlike Gabriel's "lions of lust" (120), who only serve to tear Gabriel apart, and unlike those lions to whom the prowling white men of Gabriel's town are compared (192), the lions of the library may also arm John with words, and give him strength. In John's divine vision on the threshing floor "the lion's jaws [which threatened him] were stopped" (278). John not only has words, but is also seeking the Word. As Sister McCandless observes, "The Word is hard" (72). Still, if it is hard for John, it is impossible for Gabriel, who only regards the Word as a prison:

> "Yes," [Deborah] sighed, "the Word sure do tell us that pride goes before destruction."
> "And a haughty spirit before a fall. That's the Word."
> "Yes," and she smiled again, "ain't no shelter against the Word of God, is there Reverend? You is just got to be in it, tha's all—'cause every word is true, and the gates of Hell ain't going to be able to stand against it."
> He smiled, watching her, and felt a great tenderness fill his heart. "You just *stay* in the Word, little sister." (129)

In the beginning was the Word, and the Word was with God (John 1:1), but Gabriel is not with God, nor is the Word with him. Gabriel's fundamental contradiction is that despite the fact that he is a man of God, he can never be with God, or achieve that peace of mind he associates with God. When Florence walked out on his household, Gabriel was forced to become another man who was a stranger to himself. He lived that stranger's life except for one weak moment when his life was not sterile or split in two. At that moment he became a creator. Only, he created a bastard whom he was not free to love, and who in turn was not free. It is that same bastardy which is Gabriel's as well as Roy's, the bastardy of color which Gabriel shares with John, Richard, Elisha, Elizabeth, Florence, and Frank—" 'You black bastards,' [Richard's false accuser] said, looking at him, 'You're all the same' " (232). Heaven is not open to bastards; black people have no lineage; heaven is not open to black people. If the syllogism is to be believed, then to be a black man of God is a contradiction in itself. Gabriel is father (pastor) to a bastard people who by birth are deprived of the kingdom of heaven of which he, Gabriel, is supposed to be chief angel. Standing beside that miraculous tree, Gabriel received the wrong sign; he thought he was headed for heaven, and he wound up in hell, which was a deeper hell for that discovery.

As for John, his hell is attached to Gabriel's, but it has its own peculiar characteristics as well. Like everyone else in this novel, John is searching for a father—not the miracle worker whom Gabriel seeks, but a man. The man who has been provided for him is not a father, not in the sense of being a model or example, yet in a curious way the relationship of Gabriel to John is that of guide to follower. It is evidently the same relationship which Baldwin shared with his own father, one whose familial grounding was not in love or admiration, but in a cyclical conception of history:

> The day of my father's funeral had also been my nineteenth birthday. As we drove him to the graveyard, the spoils of injustice, anarchy, discontent, and hatred were all around us [the aftermath of a Harlem race riot in the summer of 1943]. It seemed to me that God himself had devised, to mark my father's end, the most sustained and brutally dissonant of codas. And it seemed to me, too, that the violence which rose all about us as my father left the world had been devised as a corrective for the pride of his eldest son. I had declined to believe in that apocalypse which had been central to my father's vision; very well, life seemed to be saying, here is something that will certainly pass for an apocalypse until the real thing comes along. I had inclined to be contemptuous of my father for the conditions of his life, for the conditions of our lives. When his life had ended I began to wonder about that life and also, in a new way, to be apprehensive about my own. (*Notes of a Native Son*, 85–86)

There is a fine story by Jerome Weidman, "My Father Sits in the Dark," which describes the infinite distance between sons and fathers. It is about the silences they share, in which silences lie all the trusts, hopes, promises, and recriminations which a creator and his creature forever attempt to conceal from, or are unable to communicate to, each other. Weidman's story hinges on the son's exulting in the fact that, after persistent badgering, he has at last discovered why his father sits alone in the dark kitchen at night; but the truth the reader knows is that the son does not really understand why his father sits in the dark at all, nor will he ever do so. Gabriel sits in the dark of his guilt for the kitchen-floor sin, the dark of his ignorance, the dark of the shadow of his vengeful God, of his future damnation, of his aloneness, of his lovelessness, and of his people. But John has darknesses of his own. He was born out of darkness into darkness; his birthdays go uncelebrated. Like Bigger, he hides away in the camouflaging darkness of movie houses. Most of all, he lives in the darkness of his silent confusions.

He wonders if he is ugly:

> His father had always said that his face was the face of Satan—and was there not something—in the lift of the eyebrow, in the way his rough hair formed a V on his brow—that bore witness to his father's words. In the eye there was a light that was not the light of heaven, and the mouth trembled, lustful and lewd, to drink deep of the wines of Hell. He stared at his face as though it were, as indeed it soon appeared to be, the face of a stranger, a stranger who held secrets that John could never know. And, having thought of it as the face of a stranger, he tried to look at it as a stranger might, and tried to discover what other people saw. But he saw only details: two great eyes, and a broad, low forehead, and the triangle of his nose, and his enormous mouth, and the barely perceptible cleft in his chin, which was, his father said, the mark of the devil's little finger. (26–27)

Ugliness, he has learned, is to be associated with damnation, but what standards can one use to determine whether things are ugly or not? Clean things are reputed to be beautiful. He, John, is called after John the Baptist, who washed sins away. But he, called Grimes, is black himself, and as someone who is assigned to clean things, he fails: "for each dustpan he so laboriously filled at the door-sill demons added to the rug twenty more; he saw in the expanse behind him the dust that he had raised settling again into the carpet; and he gritted his teeth, already on edge because of the dust that filled his mouth, and nearly wept to think that so much labor brought so little reward" (26). His name is dirt; his house is eternally unclean, and that uncleanliness is couched in blasphemies:

> Dirt was in every corner, angle, crevice of the monstrous stove, and lived behind it in delirious communion with the corrupted wall. Dirt was in the baseboard that John scrubbed every Saturday, and roughened the cupboard shelves that held the cracked and gleaming dishes. Under this dark weight the walls leaned, under it the ceiling, with a great crack like lightning in its center, sagged. The windows gleamed like beaten gold or silver, but now John saw, in the yellow light, how fine dust veiled their doubtful glory. Dirt crawled in the gray mop hung out of the windows to dry. John thought with shame and horror, yet in angry hardness of heart: *He who is filthy, let him be filthy still.* (19)

John may be called ugly because of his "frog eyes" and oversized mouth, but, he wonders, is not everything that is black ugly? To what real beauty can John aspire except a change of skin? And since that particular conversion is not available to him, does it make any important difference to his life that his features are irregular or unpleasing to the eye? To be black is seemingly to be unlovely enough. The policemen who arrest Richard deride Elizabeth's love for Richard, because the couple is black, and love is beautiful.

John is not beautiful, and no one loves him. Not Roy, who is too fiercely intent on survival to love, nor Elizabeth, who is too fearful to love, nor Florence, whose consuming passion is the opposite of love, and certainly not Gabriel, whose God torments him. There is a single moment in *Go Tell It on the Mountain* when a kind of love flickers—the incident of John's bumping into an old man in Central Park ("the old man smiled. John smiled back" [37])—but that moment is over in a flash, and until the end of the novel, when John discovers the beginnings of brotherly love in Elisha, there is no other occurrence filled with as much pure affection. Among the others in the story, only Elizabeth and Richard truly love each other. Elisha and Ella Mae, two young people of the Temple, make a stab at love, but their love is quashed by the elders of the church because it threatens to be sexual.

One of John's most perplexing mysteries is what sex has to do with love. Everything that he learns about sex, he gets second hand. He overhears tales about his mother's father's "house." He listens to Elisha protest too much after having been shamed before the congregation for "walking disorderly" with Ella Mae, and wonders what walking disorderly means. He hears Roy, who "knew much more about such things" (4), boast about his sexual prowess. He reads words he cannot understand scribbled on walls. With Roy he watches a couple "do it standing up" (5) in an abandoned basement. And he hears his mother and father, too, rising and falling in bed in the room behind his.

Rising and falling are Christian terms, as well. Is there some connection between the sexual act and the acts of devotion, or are the two antithetical, as Gabriel insists? John falls upon the threshing floor. The question of the novel is, will he rise? He has a long distance to go. Until his moment of decision to accept the Word he had been living in a hell from which he could only escape temporarily by buying a ticket to a movie house, which like Florence's train ticket that carried her north, became a passport to him. Otherwise, he could only move laterally from one area of hell to another: the hell of his home, of his people, and of his father's God. Looking back on all three before his rise, he witnesses in revulsion the degradation of other would-be converts like himself, who groped to reach, not the Jordan, but the Styx:

> Then John saw the river, and the multitude was there. And now they had undergone a change; their robes were ragged, and stained with the road they had traveled, and stained with unholy blood; the robes of some barely covered their nakedness; and some indeed were naked. And some stumbled on the smooth stones at the river's edge, for they were blind; and some crawled with a terrrible wailing, for they were lame; some did not cease to pluck at their flesh, which was rotten with running sores. All struggled to get to the river, in a dreadful hardness of heart: the strong struck down the weak, the ragged spat on the naked, the naked cursed the blind, the blind crawled over the lame.   (276–277)

His other hell consists of his own multiple lonelinesses: the loneliness of the unloved, of the thinker who is set apart from the rest of his kind by the fact that he lives mainly in his own head, of the user of words, of the good boy whose goodness is measured by the fact that he does nothing that is not good; the loneliness of the bastard-outcast.

> I want to go through, Lord
> I want to go through.
> Take me through, Lord,
> Take me through.   (148)

Will John be able to rise out of all this mire and confusion into a new birth and deliverance?

According to Deuteronomy, the answer is no. The bastard cannot be saved despite the fact that this bastard is named for the answer to a prayer. Bastards are misfits. Yet John knows that Jesus saves. Richard calls Jesus a bastard (220). Jesus was a misfit. Richard was a misfit; like Jesus he was grouped with two thieves and died innocent.

Esther was also a misfit because of her free spirit. And John is a misfit. If he is to be classed with Jesus does it mean that he will also rise to glory? Or is it that to be a black misfit is to be a different order of outcast altogether, to be the misfit supreme, in a class by oneself? Emerson said, "Whoso would be a man must be a non-conformist." Richard, Esther, and John are nonconformists from birth, yet their nonconformity, instead of giving them pride, has in fact kept them low.

If John's lack of conformity has not made him a man, then it seems only reasonable that his manhood lies in toeing the mark. What John is doing, therefore, on that threshing floor is waiting to conform: to conform both to the expectations of everyone around him, black and white, and to that cyclical pattern which has kept all the characters in the novel from getting anywhere, while at the same time providing the illusion of mobility. John is getting nowhere on that threshing floor. No more than Elizabeth gets anywhere by repeatedly bearing children (she is pregnant again at the time of this story), the perpetually newborn. Gabriel impregnates Elizabeth as if each conception were an act of absolution, but with every new life which enters the Grimes household (read Harlem, the nation), nothing is altered except space. It is significant that the bulk of the novel is taken up by three prayers which remain unanswered and affect nothing.

On the threshing floor John falls, then he rises. He rises to the accompaniment of a mystical voice which in the guise of encouragement carries an awful threat: "you got everything your daddy got" (265). If the voice is telling the truth, and John's future is destined to become his father's past and present, then John has risen to a fall which every ensuing rise will make more steep. The spiritual "Go Tell It on the Mountain" says:

When I was a seeker
I sought both night and day
I asked the Lord to help me,
And he showed me the way.

He made me a watchman
Upon a city wall
And if I am a christian
I am the least of all.

The voice which John hears tells him to rise as if on a pilgrimage, but this voice is not the one heard by Boethius, Dante, Chaucer, or Keats in the second *Hyperion*. It is a malicious voice which advertises humility as a virtue when it means humiliation.

In the beginning John had words, but at the end, at his rise, he has run out of words: "Here there was no speech or language" (271). Elisha, also wordless at this juncture, prophesies in tongues. What he forecasts is John's salvation, but John himself cannot find the words for that event, not his own words. He calls upon Gabriel's words instead:

> John struggled to speak the authoritative, the living
> word that would conquer the great division between
> his father and himself. But it did not come, the living
> word; in the silence something died in John, and
> something came alive. It came to him that he must
> testify: his tongue only could bear witness to the
> wonders he had seen. And he remembered, suddenly,
> the text of a sermon he had once heard his father
> preach. And he opened his mouth, feeling, as he
> watched his father, the darkness roar behind him,
> and the very earth beneath him seem to shake; yet
> he gave to his father their common testimony. "I'm
> saved," he said, "and I know I'm saved." And then, as
> his father did not speak, he repeated his father's text:
> "My witness is in Heaven and my record is on
> high." (282)

The living word did not come, but his father's words came, and those words were dead. He felt something come alive in him which was death, and he felt something die in him which may have been life. Now, like his father before him, he begins to call upon signs and omens. But as he walks out of the church that morning, the skulking alley cat and gray bird he sees and the bell and siren of the ambulance he hears are signs, too, signs not of divine intervention or of a glorious multitude in unity, but of a chaotic castaway universe which is his to inherit.

Does John break the pattern laid out before him or does he fit it? Love, too, is something for which John "found no words" (299), and in Elisha he does begin to discover the capacity for love. Baldwin found that capacity at his father's funeral:

> "But as for me and my house," my father had said, "we will serve the Lord." I wondered, as we drove him to his resting place, what this line had meant for him. I had heard him preach it many times. I had preached it once myself, proudly giving it an interpretation different from my father's. Now the whole thing came back to me, as though my father and I were on our way to Sunday school and I were memorizing the golden text: *And if it seem evil unto you to serve the Lord, choose you this day whom you will serve; whether the gods which your fathers served that were on the other side of the flood, or the gods of the Amorites, in whose land ye dwell: but as for me and my house, we will serve the Lord.* I suspected in these familiar lines a meaning which had never been there for me before. All of my father's texts and songs, which I had decided were meaningless, were arranged before me at his death like empty bottles, waiting to hold the meaning which life would give them for me. This was his legacy: nothing is ever escaped. That bleakly memorable morning I hated the unbelievable streets and the Negroes and whites who had, equally, made them that way. But I knew that it was folly, as my father would have said, this bitterness was folly. It was necessary to hold on to things that mattered. The dead man mattered, the new life mattered; blackness and whiteness did not matter; to believe that they did was to acquiesce to one's own destruction. Hatred, which could destroy so much, never failed to destroy the man who hated and this was an immutable law.   (*Notes of a Native Son,* 112–113)

Lord of the Rings   53

In a sense John does break the pattern because in whatever love he achieves, he possesses something which ought to be too powerful for history. In a deeper sense, however, he fits the pattern by breaking it. Richard and Esther were destroyed by love, not hate. In a sane world, if hate destroyed the man who hated, love would restore the man who loved, and things would balance. But in a situation where everything is backward and upside down, hate destroys the hater, and love destroys the lover just as surely. This is the end, a dead one, which Baldwin foresees for John, which end was in the beginning.

Cane

Unlike that in *Go Tell It on the Mountain*, the cyclical pattern of Jean Toomer's *Cane* is not conceived of in terms of what an individual human being may strive to overcome or accomplish, but rather in terms of where that individual may be spiritually and culturally located. Like many black novels of the Harlem Renaissance, *Cane* is about the search for roots, and about the penalties a people suffers by being uprooted. All of its characters are in one way or another without a home, and the underlying, and understated, truth of the novel is that the home which the characters know full well they can never reach, but in whose existence they nevertheless wholeheartedly believe, does not exist.

Because *Cane* was pieced together from various sketches Toomer wrote over a time, there is some question as to whether the book may properly be called a novel. Certainly it is not a conventional or formal novel; not merely because it consists of apparently disconnected sketches in sequence, but because of the poems interspersed among the sketches, and the fact that "Kabnis," the major and final portion of the book, was originally conceived as a one-act play. *Cane* is, nevertheless, a novel in the sense that it conveys a self-consistent pattern. Its unity does not derive from the development of its plot or characters, but from its author's thesis.

The unity of the novel is radial, the idea of core in the book applying to the center of a nation and of a man as well. The central story (positioned in the middle of *Cane*) is "Box Seat," which deals with Dan Moore's love for a schoolteacher named Muriel. One afternoon Dan comes to call on Muriel, who lives in a boarding house owned by Mrs. Pribby, a respectable nuisance "who reads newspapers all night" (110). Muriel, too, is stiffly respectable, and during their conversation Dan tries, as he has repeatedly tried, to get both Muriel and himself to loosen up and behave more naturally with each other. They talk artificially until eight in the evening. Dan finally pleads for Muriel's love, but Muriel rebuffs him. Muriel's friend Bernice enters, and the two ladies go off to the local theater. To Bernice Muriel vows never again to see Dan because he makes her uneasy.

Dan also attends the theater that night. He is clumsy about finding his seat, disturbs the other customers, and attracts Muriel's displeased attention. The show begins. It consists of boxing dwarfs who pound each other senseless round after round to the increasing delight of the insatiable audience:

> The gong rings. No fooling this time. The dwarfs
> set to. They clinch. The referee parts them. One swings
> a cruel upper-cut and knocks the other down. A huge
> head hits the floor. Pop! The house roars. The fighter,
> groggy, scrambles up. The referee whispers to the
> contenders not to fight so hard. They ignore him.
> They charge. Their heads jab like boxing-gloves. They
> kick and spit and bite. They pound each other
> furiously. Muriel pounds. The house pounds. Cut
> lips. Bloody noses. The referee asks for the gong. Time!
> The house roars. The dwarfs bow, are made to bow.
> The house wants more. The dwarfs are led from the
> stage. (124–125)

Then one of the dwarfs, called Mr. Barry, comes back on stage singing a "sentimental love song," and holding a white rose in one hand and a mirror in the other, which he flashes in the face of everyone to whom he sings. He

Lord of the Rings 55

sings to Muriel, who recoils at the sight of him, but manages to force a smile. Mr. Barry offers the rose, now red from his own bloody nose, to Muriel, and as she falters then reluctantly accepts the offering, Dan stands and shouts, "Jesus was once a leper" (129), and starts to run from the theater. On his way out he stumbles over a man who, angered, challenges Dan to a fight outside. But by the time the two men get outside, Dan has forgotten his challenger, and keeps walking on.

Everything in the story links up with or suggests something else in the novel at large. The association of innocence with sugar cane—Dan says, "I was born in a canefield" (105)—is repeated in "Karintha" and "Fern," two of the early sketches. Time is a destructive force in "Box-Seat," as it is in the main story, "Kabnis." There is an old man in the audience whom Dan invests with prophetic powers, and the same kind of figure appears in "Kabnis" (as well as in Toomer's play, *Balo*). Particularly, there is Dan himself, like all of the men in *Cane*, out to find or prove something which perpetually seems to fly out of reach.

By walking away from the theater Dan releases himself from a kind of confinement. The theater is a "house," and in Toomer, as in Yeats, houses are instruments of constriction. The sketch that immediately precedes "Box-Seat" is called "Theater." It is about a man, John, so narrowly confined by convention that he has lost the ability to love. At Mrs. Pribby's, Dan feels that "the house contracts about him." It seems that he is bolted, "bolted to the endless rows of metal houses" (107), which are compared to prison cells. In the theater Dan thinks that "the seats are bolted houses" (117). Muriel's own house is described as a fortress, and at the beginning of the story Dan wonders how it would be to break into this house, just as he wonders if he can break through the emotional fortifications which Muriel has built for herself against him. The story of "Rhobert," the second piece in the second section of *Cane*, is about a man who "wears a house, like a monstrous diver's helmet, on his head" (73). Muriel's house is worn on her heart, and the house she wears expands continually. Emblematic of a force or instrument which deprives people of free movement, it is like the theater "house" in response to the battling dwarfs; it roars and wants more.

The dwarfs themselves are brutalized people, trained to translate their brutalization into an evening's entertainment. Their act is akin to the battle royal in *Invisible Man*; the savagery of the dwarfs is meant to amuse an audience which already had to have reached a savage condition and level of apprehension in order to regard the dwarfs as amusing. The fact that the black audience cheers on the dwarfs perpetuates a cycle of brutality in which each group of the downtrodden seeks only to find solace or satisfaction in the humiliation of another. The dwarfs remind us of the dwarfs who taunted Samson. They provide not high theater but melodrama (Mr. Barry sings a sentimental song and holds a rose). The name of the theater in which the action takes place, the action on stage and the internal action of Dan's mind, is The Lincoln, thus yoking the ideal of freedom to a grim reality. Freedom in "Box-Seat" is cheap theater, a side-show, and the theater house itself is less of a playhouse than a theater of war.

When the dwarf holds the mirror to the faces of the audience he is saying, see yourself in me. The dwarfs in fact have counterparts throughout *Cane*; all the black characters in the novel must, in order to survive, conduct themselves according to dangerous, cruel, false, or ludicrous standards. For a member of that audience to look at his own image in the dwarf's mirror is to behold himself in the dwarf's hands, which are the hands of the misfit, the freak. Dan, like John Grimes, can readily accept the idea of being an outcast in the context of that theater, because he does not want to be accepted in an audience which has falsified its nature:

> He shrivels close beside a portly Negress whose huge rolls of flesh meet about the bones of seat-arms.
> A soil-soaked fragrance comes from her. Through the

cement floor her strong roots sink down. They spread under the asphalt streets. Dreaming, the streets roll over on their bellies, and suck their glossy health from them. Her strong roots sink down and spread under the river and disappear in blood-lines that waver south. Her roots shoot down. Dan's hands follow them. Roots throb. Dan's heart beats violently. He places his palms upon the earth to cool them. Earth throbs. Dan's heart beats violently. He sees all the people in the house rush to the walls to listen to the rumble. A new-world Christ is coming up. Dan comes up. He is startled. The eyes of the woman don't belong to her. They look at him unpleasantly. From either aisle, bolted masses press in. He doesn't fit. (119)

But for Muriel the reflection in the dwarf's hands intimates an alliance which is too awful to bear. It is particularly unbearable to her that the mirror should suggest a total reversal of aesthetic and moral value, a reversal which the bloody dwarf himself, as entertainer, effectively represents. Dan cries out that Jesus was once a leper, not meaning that the dwarf should be considered to be Jesus reborn, but simply that his deformity is a sign of his common humanity, and only becomes an aberration when abused, or if the observer wishes him to be so. In a way, the dwarf could serve as a Christ to Muriel if she were able to surmount her revulsion and open her heart, but Muriel is too far gone. As Muriel and Dan chatted at Mrs. Pribby's, Dan noticed that "the houses, the rows of houses, locked about her chair" (113).

Muriel is in a box, as are Mrs. Pribby, Bernice, and the crowd at the theater. The title, "Box-Seat," refers to entrapment: a seat within a box, a seat that is a box, a seat at a boxing match. In the final section of the novel, "Kabnis," the church windows are described as being "box like" (169), because the church has only provided suffocation for everyone in that story. "Box" is a slang term for coffin. All of the characters in "Box-Seat" are dead spiritually, except for Dan, and even Dan only barely manages to escape with his "life." Whether he also escapes with his sanity is another question. The theater he flees is a madhouse whose occupants call his own behavior crazy. Dan acts like a lunatic in order to escape the madhouse, but we know nothing of the true state of his mind at the end of the story. As he walks away from the fight, has he reached some new and clear understanding of himself, or is he now simply stunned or lost totally? Is he heading somewhere or merely away?

Dan takes his name from the biblical king, and the naming is patently ironic. In the Bible nothing is known of Daniel's parentage or lineage, and nothing is known of this Dan's family tree either. He derogates himself by thinking that as he bangs on Muriel's front door, he may be mistaken by neighbors for a baboon, and he accepts the association willingly, implying that if real trees are to be considered his family trees, he will hurl the notion of his being ape-like back into the faces of his zoo-keepers: "Give me your fingers and I will peel them as if they were ripe bananas" (106). Like King Daniel, Dan has no roots, with the difference that Dan's roots were yanked out from under him and that he was deprived of a genealogy by commerce. The name Daniel means "a judge is God," but in "Box-Seat" it is everyone else who judges Daniel, and it is Dan who is weighed in the distorted balance and found wanting. King Daniel was a great interpreter of dreams who could read the handwriting on the wall. Dan is an interpreter of lost dreams. He reads his fate in the theater performance, and like his namesake, he too flees the lion's den, but in so doing he is hailed as a fool, not a king. The book of Daniel is apocalyptic literature; here the apocalypse has been reduced to a pair of dwarfs at each other's throats.

All of the biblical references in *Cane* have the same bitter edge to them. In the Bible Rebekah was the beautiful virgin who married Isaac, the promising son. Her own two sons, Jacob and Esau, came, as with Elisabeth and Zacharias, in answer to a prayer against barrenness: "And the Lord said unto her, Two nations are in thy womb, and two manner of people shall be separated from thy bowels" (Genesis 25:23). In *Cane*, Becky is a white woman expelled from her town because she bears a black man's son. Five years later she has another boy, and no one knows if the children are white or black: "No one knew, and least of all themselves" (11). Eventually people hear that "they drifted around from job to job. We, who had cast out their mother because of them, could we take them in? They answered black and white folks by shooting up two men and leaving town. 'Godam the white folks; godam the niggers,' they shouted as they left town" (11). Like Rebekah, Becky was involved with two warring nations, but both nations rejected her. She dies alone when the roof of her cabin caves in, and in a final act of pity or reverence the townspeople toss a Bible on the pile of rubbish.

Esther of the Old Testament was the fierce queen who saved her people from a massacre. Toomer's Esther ("Esther") is a pretentious near-white girl, scorned by the coal black "King Barlo" because she does not know who her people are. Saul saw a vision of Jesus which changed his life. Toomer's Paul ("Bona and Paul"), who can pass for white, has no idea which way to convert, or what to change in himself. John the Baptist was known for his protest against the luxury of his age; John the Evangelist, for his impetuosity. Toomer's John ("Theater") cannot deal with his passion for the dancer, Dorris. He is tightly locked into the luxuries of his age, and is afraid to love.

Dan is related to Paul and John, and to every man in *Cane*, because all of the men in the book share the condition of threatened or actual emasculation. In the same way, Muriel is related to the book's women, because almost all of them share the condition of having lost their spirit or pride. The women in Part I, Karintha, Becky, Carma, Fern, Esther, and Louisa, are all close to the roots in Southern soil, but these women have been transplanted, and the American soil on which they are located is not really theirs. The women in Part II, Avey, Dorris, and Muriel, are city girls, the more dramatically uprooted, the housed and boxed in. The men and women in all of the sketches are related to each other by the interspersed poems, whose themes connect each immediately preceding sketch to the one that follows. The controlling connections, between all parts of *Cane*, are made in Part III, "Kabnis." As "Box-Seat" is the center of the circle, "Kabnis" is the outer rim.

"Kabnis" takes the setting of *Cane* away from the city, and back to Georgia. Ralph Kabnis is an ex-schoolteacher full of self-disgust, boredom, and hatred who spends his days cursing his fate and wishing for "an ugly world" (161). He believes that he is going mad and tries to talk himself out of it: "Come, Ralph, pull yourself together. Curses and adoration dont come from what is sane. This loneliness, dumbness, awful, intangible oppression is enough to drive a man insane. Miles from nowhere. A speck on a Georgia hillside. Jesus, can you imagine it—an atom of dust in agony on a hillside? That's a spectacle for you. Come, Ralph, old man, pull yourself together" (162). Recently returned from the North, Kabnis becomes part of the local scene. He takes a job teaching school again, but is fired for being drunk, and ends up working as a clean-up boy in Fred Halsey's store. To kill more time, he spends hours talking at an old recluse called Father John who lives in Halsey's basement. The old man has not spoken a word for years, but one night when a party has degenerated into an orgy and then died out entirely Father John mutters about the "sin th white folks 'mitted when they made the Bible lie" (237). Hearing this, Kabnis, infuriated that the old man's revelation should turn out to be such a commonplace, calls him a "black fakir," then falls to his knees drunk and exhausted. In the end he has to be led upstairs and out into the morning by Carrie K., Halsey's daughter.

Pull yourself together, Ralph tells himself, but the task is impossible. He can neither pull himself together in terms of his personal momentary well-being, nor pull himself together culturally or historically in the name of his people. He is the epitome of the disoriented man. In *Essentials*, his book of aphorisms, Toomer called man generally "a nerve of the cosmos, dislocated, trying to quiver into place." Kabnis claims that curses and adoration do not come from what is sane, but it is not so. Only in a disoriented world is sanity defined by the absences of mysteries or passions, and Kabnis occupies, and in a way constitutes, such a world. He is correctly referred to as a "completely artificial man" (263). The fact that he has been a schoolteacher (Muriel is also a schoolteacher) and a man of learning only increases the despair of his dislocations. Education has done nothing for Kabnis, who has no sense of being, no identifiable center for education to build on.

The old man says, "O th sin th white folks 'mitted when they made th Bible lie" (237), and Kabnis is furious because he knew it all along. From the old man to whom he turned as to a prophet, he sought some new and different revelation—a way out—but what he got instead was the same old story, not that the Bible lied, but that it was *made* to lie. There is the sin, and the horror: the deliberate perversion of what ought to have served as beauty and truth into an instrument of oppression and humiliation. The juxtaposition in the story of the terrible tale of the pregnant black woman killed in the streets by white men, her stomach slit open, her new-born child pinned to a tree, and the episode of the Sister of the church crying, "Jesus, Jesus, I've found Jesus" (179), makes sense in its irony. It is only natural that Kabnis sees the church as box-like; he sees the church as having brought him and his people more death than redemption. As the sister continues to sing, a rock crashes through the church window with a note wrapped around it: "You northern nigger, its time fer y t leave. Git along now" (179).

But there is no place for Kabnis to go. He has progressed, as *Cane* itself has progressed, from south to north, back south again, without ever finding roots or a core, a sense of place, or self. The local girls preening themselves before the mirror for the orgy are compared to African princesses, but the comparison is invidious and empty. In another country these girls might indeed have been princesses, but as Countee Cullen's poem suggested, what is Africa now to these girls whose hair "has gone through some straightening process," and whose ancestry has been obscured? All that remains for them is to lie with men like Halsey and Kabnis, who are, like themselves, in every way impotent.

In "Carma," Toomer said that "the Dixie Pike has grown from a goat path in Africa" (18). What the novel proves, however, is that the goat path is long overgrown and hidden. For people such as Dan, Muriel, and Kabnis, all there is to rely on is the repetition of loss: "Do y think youre out of slavery? Huh?" Kabnis asks the old man.

> Youre where they used t throw th worked-out,
> no-count slaves. On a damp clammy floor of a dark
> scum-hole. An they called that an infirmary. Th
> sons-a . . . . Why I can already see you toppled off
> that stool an stretched out on th floor beside me—
> not beside me, damn you, by yourself, with the flies
> buzzin an lickin God knows what they'd find on a
> dirty, black, foul-breathed mouth likc yours. (233)

Kabnis' harangue is equally meant for himself. When he was saying pull yourself together Ralph, he called himself "old man."

The title *Cane* refers to roots. In a pamphlet Toomer once wrote for the Society of Friends ("The Flavor of Man"), he said, "A man's roots must go down into what is deeper than himself, his crown touch what is higher, his heart open to the beyond, and the whole move forward. Then he will be connected with the great heart and power of life." The title refers to the idea of support as well. All of the characters in *Cane* vainly seek a cane or something to lean on. But there may be a deeper pun here, too. Cain and Abel were the sons of Eve, equal at their births except that by divine caprice or mystery Cain was automatically rejected by God and Abel was the favored boy. Abel could talk with God, but Cain did not even have Abel to talk with, and when Cain finally killed his brother, after his own offerings to God had been refused, God placed a mark on Cain so that he might be known to suffer eternal punishment. Genesis says then that "Cain went out of the presence of the Lord," but even while Abel had lived, Cain had not enjoyed that presence. For no reason but an accident of birth Cain, like Kabnis, had always been a fugitive.

In *Native Son* the cycle is societal, in *Go Tell It on the*

Mountain it is hereditary, and here it is largely cultural and spiritual. In all three novels, escape from a cyclical pattern is conceived of in terms of regeneration, but for the characters involved regeneration means only repetition, and to be reborn is part of a process of damnation. Nevertheless, at one point Kabnis exclaims, "Great God Almighty, a soul like mine cant pin itself onto a wagon wheel an satisfy itself in spinnin round" (234). He shows great surprise in this. With him, as with Bigger and John Grimes, there is the sense that he suffers a predicament he cannot believe, that he has been caught in a pattern of life belonging to someone else.

That this is true, and that the someone else is he, only aggravate Kabnis' disunity. The superficial fragmentation of *Cane* is meant to reflect that disunity, and despite the radial structure in which the coherence of the novel may be found, Toomer is presenting us here with a number of characters whose only sense of personal cohesion derives from their attachment to historical inevitabilities. The same may be said of Baldwin, Wright, and the great majority of black authors, who rely on the cyclical conception of black American history as a backdrop, and sometimes support, to the eccentricities of their heroes. They not only use that conception as a technical framework, but often a substitute for fate.

As is the case with black fiction generally, the Bible and aspects of Christian doctrine play an important role in these novels, particularly as literary referents; but they do not control the books in the sense of providing reasons for action or explanations of thought. Such reasons and explanations depend rather on each author's traditionalist belief that the future of his story lies in the past. What this judgment, which is a form of insurance, creates in turn is the kind of backward progression mentioned earlier, in which a character seems to oppose the direction of a historical cycle when he is in fact reinforcing it. Remarkably, then, both the chaotic element in and the stable condition of the literature are traceable to the consistency of the same delusion.

2
Eccentricities

She was sixteen. She had glossy leaves and bursting buds and she wanted to struggle with life but it seemed to elude her. Where were the singing bees for her? Nothing on the place nor in her grandma's house answered her. She searched as much of the world as she could from the top of the front steps and then went on down to the front gate and leaned over to gaze up and down the road. Looking, waiting, breathing short with impatience. Waiting for the world to be made.

—Zora Neale Hurston, *Their Eyes Were Watching God*

The idea that most of black fiction is made up of patterns of cyclical history has little to do with its success as literature. It is not the reasonable suspicion that John Grimes will follow in his father's footsteps which engages the reader's attention, but rather the hope that John may take a different route. Similarly, although it is certain that Carrie K. is leading Kabnis nowhere at the end of *Cane*, the reader must hope, if only because we customarily regard ascensions as hopeful, that the two miserable characters moving up that flight of basement stairs will find a better house at the top. In both instances and many more in black writing, hope is not merely the instrument by which interest is maintained or tension developed, but also a way by which a character's humanity can be delineated within the context of a seemingly mechanical situation. Hope means the hope of escape from a cycle, and people are characterized by the method they choose.

The theme of religion would seem to offer the greatest promise for an individual's breaking of historical patterns, and for self-assertion, but it does not. As is the case with other contradictions in the literature, the reason for this may be directly traced to a contradiction in aesthetics. Blake's black boy protests that his soul is white, meaning that the part of him essential to paradise is sanctified, even if the rest of him is damned. The rationale for calling white the right color is not only that white is considered to be beautiful in itself, but that it is also a portion, reflection, or model of a larger scheme which is ultimate beauty. Call that scheme heaven, its founder God, and the connection between cleanliness (whiteness) and godliness is inevitable. Plotinus' tractate on beauty made a neat package of suiting the "Forming-Idea" to the coordination of the parts and the sum; Wordsworth had his sublime sense of the deeply interfused; Coleridge's standard for a supreme work of art was that it exhibit "multitude in unity." As great as such a multitude is, as great as is the diversity, it can only include those things that may be properly defined as beautiful. In a world equipped with predetermined definitions of beauty, black is out of it. It is not merely the color of the exile or outcast in a sociological or economic sense; it is also, in spiritual terms, the color of eccentricity, incoherence, and disharmony.

Religious symbols in black fiction, therefore, are almost always double-edged. The cross that the preacher gives to Bigger is no different in Bigger's sight from the crosses that the mob is burning outside his jail. The Bible that Gabriel uses as a sledgehammer, and women like Bigger's mother and Aunt Hager of Langston Hughes's *Not Without Laughter* depend on for solace, is the same Bible that in *Cane* flapped "its leaves with an aimless rustle" (13) on Becky's funeral mound after the town had expelled her for miscegenation. The Bible's white-saved, black-damned associations, particularly in Matthew, Lamentations, Isaiah, and Psalms, work against the characters' trust in it. Biblical stories are often altered to illustrate this sense of defeat. Arna Bontemps' *Black Thunder* is the account of a quashed slave rebellion in which most of the characters bear apt Biblical names, including a slave named Pharaoh, who betrays the rebellion, and sees to it that no exodus occurs.

As for God Himself, though always depicted as the Christian God, He is not benign, but vengeful and capricious. In Zora Neale Hurston's *Their Eyes Were Watching God*, for example, God is fearful: "They sat in company with the others in other shanties, their eyes straining against crude walls and their souls asking if He meant to measure their puny might against His" (131). Moreover, God's power has a special quality to it. The characters of the novel refer to God as "Big Massa" and "Ole Massa," indicating that for all their piety they still conceive of religion as a giant plantation system with heaven as the big house and themselves in the fields. At an early point in the book Miss Hurston declares, "All Gods who receive homage are cruel. All gods dispense suffering without reason. Otherwise they would not be worshipped. Through indiscriminate suffering men know fear and fear is the most divine emotion. It is the stones for altars and the beginning of wisdom. Half gods are worshipped in wine and flowers. Real gods require blood" (120).

Under such circumstances, salvation becomes a desperate notion. Aunt Hager may sing of the "Stars Beyond" and the by and by, Mrs. Thomas may sing of making the successful run from the cradle to the grave, but Bigger belittles such hopes with his own existence:

> "Didn't you know that the penalty for killing that white woman would be death?"
> "Yeah; I knew it. But I felt like she was killing me, so I didn't care."
> "If you could be happy in religion now, would you want to be?"
> "Naw. I'll be dead soon enough. If I was religious, I'd be dead now."
> "But the church promises eternal life?"
> "That's for whipped folks."   (330)

When John Grimes gets the Word and cries "I'm saved," it's a cry of recognition of his relationship with his father, and not of his future place in heaven. In *Manchild in the Promised Land*, Claude Brown asked, "Where does one run to when he's already in the promised land?" (viii), meaning Harlem. Du Bois' smoke king carved "God in night" and painted "hell in white." Bigger says that he has no soul.

Although the idea of hope attached to religion, or specifically to the Christian doctrine, finds expression in practically every black novel in one form or another, no story is totally built around such hope. Furthermore, wherever Christian devotion is expressed, it is almost always repudiated with authority. Usually the most deeply religious characters in black fiction are the elderly, whom the author ordinarily depicts as being strong in terms of stamina, but also ignorant, and therefore having a greater need for faith and superstition. Even in *Go Tell It on the Mountain*, where Christianity is practiced passionately by young and old alike, one senses religion to be a sustaining force only in the lives of the elders of the church, the Sisters who, like Bigger's mother, are closest in time and feeling to the old days.

Yet if the theme of religion has been superannuated as a source of hope in the literature, there are other themes, around which entire stories and characters are built, that recur repeatedly. These are the themes of childhood, education, love, and primitivism, each of which proffers the same kind of salvation traditionally ascribed to Christianity, namely, redemption and equality under God. All of them, like Christianity, seem in the end to be judged a failure, but for the writer who inspires his characters with one or another of these sources of hope, the foreknowledge of failure, both on his own part and on the part of his readers, is a useful device. The assurance of disappointment or disaster assures in turn the intensity of the force which opposes it, which is the beginning of tragedy.

"Big Boy Leaves Home"

Every story that deals with childhood in black fiction is in a sense an escape story, because the condition of childhood itself suggests a method of escape from, or avoidance of, the adult, and dangerous, world. The simple act of starting out on a new and unblemished life is almost by definition a hopeful enterprise, and the children in black fiction, more so than elsewhere, are always thought to be capable of fulfilling promises of a brighter dawn. When a writer such as Toomer wishes to underscore his wasteland theme, he will assign special roles to the children. It is no accident that every child who acts or is alluded to in *Cane* is either deformed, crazy, tortured, or killed. Nor is it merely a function of plot that Bigger considers murdering Buddy, that Cross Damon at the end of Wright's *The Outsider* denies the existence of his own son, or that Leona in Baldwin's *Another Country* is unable to bear children.

In the short story "Big Boy Leaves Home" (*Uncle Tom's Children*), Wright made use of childhood as a potential escape mechanism by setting the mechanism within an escape story of a different kind. At the outset Big Boy Morrison and his three young friends are free and full of their own innocence. They sing together, joke, tussle with each other, and cling to the earth as if they fused with it:

> They fell silent, smiling, dropping the lids of
> their eyes softly against the sunlight.
>   "Man, don the groun feel warm?"
>   "Jus lika bed."
>   "Jeeesus, Ah could stay here ferever."
>   "Me too."
>   "Ah kin feel tha ol sun goin all thu me."
>   "Feels like mah bones is warm."   (18–19)

When they decide to ignore a No Trespassin' sign and to head for a white man's forbidden swimming hole, they appear to have crossed over into Eden:

> They grew pensive. A black winged butterfly
> hovered at the water's edge. A bee droned. From
> somewhere came the sweet scent of honeysuckles.
> Dimly they could hear sparrows twittering in the
> woods. They rolled from side to side, letting sunshine
> dry their skins and warm their blood. They plucked
> blades of grass and chewed them.   (27)

At that moment, however, a white woman comes upon the scene and Paradise is lost. Big Boy and his friends are naked in the water. In order to retrieve their clothes they must go where the white woman is standing. She backs off terrified as the boys approach. Her fiancé, an army officer in uniform, rushes to the rescue, gun in hand. Immediately he kills one boy, then two. Big Boy and Bobo, the two who remain, wrestle the rifle out of the soldier's hands, and when the soldier lunges for the weapon, Big Boy kills him.

Now the manhunt begins. Big Boy and Bobo split up, Big Boy returning to his home. When his parents hear what has happened they are as terrified and desperate for their community, fearing reprisals, as they are for their son. After much questioning and consultation, they decide that Big Boy should hide overnight in one of a number of recently constructed kilns, there to wait until Will Sanders can pick him up in his truck and transport him to Chicago. Big Boy follows instructions, and hides and waits, hoping that Bobo will join him. After having to kill a snake in order to secure his hiding place, he dreams of lashing out at those who put him in the kiln:

> He jerked another blade and chewed. Yeah, ef Pa had
> only let im have tha shotgun! He could stan off a
> whole mob wid a shotgun. He looked at the ground
> as he turned a shotgun over in his hands. Then he
> levelled it at an advancing white man. *Boooom!*
> The man curled up. Another came. He reloaded
> quickly, and let him have what the other had got.
> He too curled up. Then another came. He got the same
> medicine. Then the whole mob swirled around him,
> and he blazed away, getting as many as he could. They
> closed in; but, by Gawd, he had done his part, hadn't
> he? N the newspaperd say: NIGGER KILLS DOZEN
> OF MOB BEFO LYNCHED! Er mabbe theyd say:
> TRAPPED NIGGER SLAYS TWENTY BEFO
> KILLED! He smiled a little. Tha wouldn't be so bad,
> would it? Blinking the newspaper away, he looked
> over the fields.   (44)

Finally he hears the voices of his white pursuers, shouting in celebration that Big Boy's home has been burned to the ground. Then from his vantage point he watches the towns-people discover and capture Bobo, dismember his body, and tar and feather the remains. A dog comes upon Big Boy, and Big Boy strangles it. In the morning he lies in the bottom of Will Sanders' truck, making his escape.

In the beginning was innocence, and at the end was experience, but it was a black child's experience, not a universal experience. When the boys started out in the morning, everything was mysterious and hopeful. Big Boy was a recognizable romantic hero, leading his would-be Sancho Panzas, talking of the excitement of trains, of getting somewhere, and being "bound for glory"(19). Even nature conspired with him—until he and his friends trespassed on the white man's territory, and all mysteries were resolved. Once the boys had ventured beyond their prescribed limitations, geographical and otherwise, everything worked against them, as if by grand design. The astonished white woman, so astonished that she could not even mutter a word of explanation when her fiancé asked, "You hurt, Bertha, you hurt?" (29) might have moved away from the boys instead of backing off to the exact spot where the clothing lay. Instead, she positioned herself so as to make death inevitable: "Yuh see, Pa, she was standin' right *by* our cloes; n when we went t git em she jus screamed" (34). Dressed in white, and white herself, the woman was the standard emblem of virginity. The mere presence of blackness in Eden was enough to defile her.

Operating on a sexual fantasy which was the product of an inherited sexual guilt, the townspeople wreaked a revenge which was also sexual in character. Dan McCall has pointed out in his discussion of this story (in *The Example of Richard Wright*) that Bobo's dismembering and tar and feathering are described as though the witnesses were experiencing mass sexual intercourse. It is a rape of Bobo that is being perpetrated as well as murder, a rape which occurs within a distorted context of American history, in which a black man has become a kind of frontier for the depravity of the mob. Here is the imported savage brought before the colonists who had required savages to indicate their own superiority, and had run out of their supply. Without defenses, Bobo becomes a frontier for sin, someone on whom to test, as if in a pioneering venture, the depths of human degradation. Sheer terror of revenge had built up the accusation of rape for Bigger, and that same terror creates the accusation of rape in the minds of Bobo's lynchers. Bobo is dismembered because of that terror, which is a terror of self.

Big Boy pays close attention to the dismembering. It provides part of his education, just as before the killing of the soldier aspects of a more innocent life provided a different education. Big Boy's story, after all, despite the thrust of its violence, is simply a tale of American boyhood: the adventures of a Huck Finn or Holden Caulfield who plays hooky in order to cull his education from the great wide world, and who disparages book-learning as being impractical. When Big Boy tells his father what happened in the woods, his father's anger is initially aroused by the discovery that Big Boy did not go to school that day, his implication being that a formal education provided a certain order for his son (John Grimes is advised to "stay in the Word"), and that that order would keep Big Boy safe. It is in a different order, however, that Big Boy acquires his real education, and what begins as the story of a budding romantic ends in the creation of a realist.

Yet at heart Big Boy is no more realistic as a result of his adventure than he was before the adventure occurred. His dream of revenge and power is fully as romantic as any of his former dreams; only the scope has changed. Now, instead of seeing things in a haze, he has a terrible clarity of vision. As the story itself has shifted to a kind of naturalism and grown "harder," so Big Boy hardens, which is a sign of his manhood. Growing up in this story (as it is in Ernest Gaines's "The Sky Is Gray" and Wright's "Almos' a Man") is accompanied by a decrease in feeling. Like Wright himself in *Black Boy*, Big Boy matures through a toughening and narrowing of the spirit.

Otherwise, Big Boy fits the pattern of the American boyhood hero in almost every way. He is big, blustering, at least at the start, and he becomes a leader of others through the force of his natural energy and cunning. He is equipped with valuable folk wisdom, and shows his friends

how to win a fight when the odds are against them. Like
Silas, Mann, and Taylor of the other stories in *Uncle Tom's
Children*, he is an individual who must win as one against
the many. A true hero, he is brave, resourceful, and innocent as well, singing songs about sexual activity which he
does not understand. At the end he is off to another
promised land, intending to live by his own independent
values.

Yet there is another pattern of heroism being worked out
in the story which undercuts Big Boy's heroics. The white
man who kills, and is killed in turn, is also a hero, a soldier
in uniform who, like Big Boy, fights against the odds (four
to one), and loses with valor. His woman in white is a
heroine as well, not to be harmed or forsaken. And the
mob, in smoking out Bobo, displays the same kind of
wisdom Big Boy expounded: "Yuh see, when a ganga guys
jump on yuh, all yuh gotta do is put the heat on one of
them n make im tell the others t let up" (23).

Between the two patterns of heroism there can be no
contest. History and numbers have insured the fact that the
white heroism will drive out the black. Even the parody Big
Boy and the others sing at the beginning of the story foreshadows Big Boy's defeat:

> Bye n bye
> Ah wanna piece of pie
> Pies too sweet
> Ah wanna piece of meat
> Meats too red
> Ah wanna piece of bread
> Breads too brown
> Ah wanna go t town
> Towns too far
> Ah wanna ketch a car
> Cars too fas
> Ah fall n break mah ass
> Ahll understand it better bye n bye.   (22)

At the outset Big Boy does crave something sweet, a peach
cobbler. The white woman imagines that it is she who is the

"piece of meat" he wants. The meat is "too red," the incident ending in bloodshed. Big Boy does get his bread, a gift from his mother. He does want to go to town (Chicago). He has to catch a fast truck. And as for whether he will understand it better bye and bye, that, as it does in the song, remains a question.

Big Boy's youth and freedom in the beginning seemed to indicate that the cyclical pattern would be broken, but the cycle assumed and overwhelmed that sense of hope and made it futile. The story is entitled "Big Boy Leaves Home," and when Big Boy does leave home the scene is an archetype of the American boy going away from his reluctant but understanding family to seek his fortune in the world outside. Big Boy's mother gives him bread, his father gives advice, and the prodigal son is off to the Land of Plenty. At the end Big Boy has escaped from the mob, and it is this escape for which the reader has been hoping all along. Yet when the event finally happens there is no sense of relief. There are other mobs waiting in Chicago, and Chicago will represent a broken promise just as Big Boy does himself. All his innocence and exuberance were simply not enough to prevent Big Boy from becoming Bigger.

Not Without Laughter

> "Cross, you aint never said how come you was reading all them books," Joe pointed out.
> "I was looking for something," Cross said quietly.
> "What?" Pink asked.
> "I don't know," Cross confessed gloomily.
> "Did you find it?" Joe asked.
> "No."
>
> —Richard Wright, The Outsider

In Not Without Laughter, despite the implication of the title, the potential means of breaking a cyclical pattern is education, education both in a formal sense and as it applies to the acquisition of an intelligence capable of dealing with a system which regularly works to domesticate it. Sandy Williams is a boy of promise, like John Grimes or

Big Boy, who in the hopes of his family is supposed to get somewhere, to rise, which in fact he does. At the end of the novel, with the help of his mother and sister, Sandy is set to go off to college and save his soul. But until he reaches that point, he has already been educated by a number of looser forces, which have attended him with greater constancy and strength than his school curriculum. The questions which Hughes implies in this book are whether the two kinds of education, the academic and worldly, are equally valuable to a black child, whether they are equally valid, whether either one alone is valid or valuable, whether they are compatible, antithetical, or mutually exclusive.

These questions arise continually in black fiction, and are not easily answered. Du Bois' John ("Of the Coming of John"), Johnson's Ex-Colored Man, Ellison's Invisible Man, Himes's Bob Jones, Kabnis, Thurman's Emma Lou Morgan, (*The Blacker the Berry*), and others all try college with painful results; yet the untutored intelligences of these characters, which they demonstrated either to show themselves worthy of college, or after they had been disillusioned by it, proved to be no more useful or satisfying to them than the academies. The crisis of their education, and of Sandy's, comes down to the fundamental problem in this literature of whether the act of learning, formal or otherwise, is an act of improvement. If the answer to that question seems to be no, the absence of an alternative suggests a terrible kind of self-denial. In order to survive in a white situation, a black character will often deliberately demean or minimize his intellectual capabilities, and eventually isolate himself from his own mind.

The three forces which influence Sandy before his schooling begins are Christianity, music, and laughter, all of which interrelate and occasionally become confused. The spokesman for Christianity in the book is Aunt Hager Williams, Sandy's grandmother and the mother of his mother, Anjee. Hager is a former slave whose enormous strength of will provides the novel with its force of gravity. There is no doubt or ambiguity in her Christian devotion.

Of all the book's characters it is she who has had the most difficult time, yet she only speaks of doing the Lord's work, being the Lord's help, and praising His name, basing her faith firmly on the negative principle that as bad as things may be, they would be worse without religion. Her youngest daughter, Harriet, Sandy's aunt, remains unconvinced of this principle, and eventually deserts the household to keep company with other young people of the town, whom Hager considers godless. When Hager pleads, "I just want you to grow up decent, chile," Harriet cries, "lemme go! You old Christian fool!" (49), and accuses her grandmother of trusting in a white Jesus, He who "don't like niggers" (45).

Whether or not Hager understands the accusation, the hallmarks of her Christianity are all oriented toward a white world. Expressing an inherited white sense of aesthetics, she continually speaks in terms of achieving the light of God, and refers to cleansing one's soul in preparation for salvation. Her occupation is washing clothes; yet she also seems forever to be scrubbing and polishing, as if in an effort to make amends for her own blackness. Hager has fully absorbed the Protestant ethic. She disapproves of the intellectual and social pretensions of her well-heeled daughter Tempy, yet she equally disapproves of Anjee's husband, Jimboy, of his singing, freedom, and lack of seriousness. Hager believes in joylessness and obedience, and will work herself to death, as indeed she does, in order to get to heaven. One night when Harriet has sneaked out to a dance, Hager waits up for her holding in her hands a Bible and a switch, the two symbols of her faith.

Sandy observes Hager's religiosity as he observes everything in the first half of the novel, without comment. He functions largely as a photographic plate, on which a number of different impressions are made, but gives no sign of what effect those impressions may be having. He has only two direct run-ins with Christianity himself: once when he gets out of attending a revival meeting so that he can go to a carnival; and again when he pockets a nickel given to him for the Sunday School collection basket in order to buy candy. Hager exclaims, "de idee o' withholdin' yo' Sunday

School money from de Lawd," but Sandy's deeper punishment comes from his father's "I'm ashamed of you" (127). Sandy suffers because he violated human ethics, not because he stole from the Lord. By the time he enters school, he does not really know if he is Christian or not.

Sandy gets his music from the blues which Jimboy and Harriet sing and dance to. Music in *Not Without Laughter* functions partly as a narcotic, but each of the songs in the book, like the original slave songs, contains a sober or practical undercurrent. Occasionally the music gets out of control, and the undercurrent overwhelms the sound. At the dance Harriet attends, the four black men in "Benbow's wandering band" were

> exploring depths to which mere sound had no
> business to go. Cruel, desolate, unadorned was their
> music now, like the body of a ravished woman on
> the sun-baked earth; violent and hard, like a giant
> standing over his bleeding mate in the blazing sun.
> The odors of bodies, the stings of flesh, and the utter
> emptiness of soul when all is done—these things
> the piano and the drums, the cornet and the twanging
> banjo insisted on hoarsely to a beat that made the
> dancers move, in that little hall, like pawns on a
> frenetic checker board.   (97)

The music is described in similes of violence and fate, both of which usually play beneath the surface of blues lyrics, and which attend Jimboy's and Harriet's lives throughout the story. Sandy merely listens pleased to the music around him, and does not participate in it, but in the first pages of the book, Hughes hints at the more sinister effects of music on the boy. In the wake of the opening hurricane, "Sandy saw a piano flat on its back in the grass. Its ivory keys gleamed in the moonlight like grinning teeth, and the strange sight made his little body shiver" (8).

Laughter, the third force which operates on Sandy, is the most conspicuous and consistent of the three. There is always a great deal of laughing going on in this novel, Jimboy's and Harriet's especially. Harriet's boyfriend is described in terms of his grin; Maudel, the town madame, is forever laughing; during the dance "a ribbon of laughter swirled round the hall" (95). There is much ridiculous activity in the story as well, particularly the absurb projects of Hager's church, which presents a pageant called "The Drill of All Nations," in which Anjee plays Sweden. Laughter is also connected with music, as in the image of the grinning piano. In Hughes's description of the band, the banjo is cynical, the drums are flippant, and the cornet laughs.

The reason for this connection is that both laughter and music are instruments of desolation in the novel, the more so for their conventional and hypothetical associations with joy. The townspeople's amusement at the antics of the freaks in the carnival is hollow and mirthless, as was the reaction of the audience to the boxing dwarfs in *Cane*. Here, as in *Cane*, as in Eliot's "Hysteria," there is a fierce desperation behind everything which is theoretically funny. Jimboy finds momentary companionship with the carnival's Fat Lady because he knows that in another context he too is a freak. He also senses that he and Sandy in the audience have a kinship with the act they watch: Sambo and Rastus, "the world's funniest comedians," who perform on a plantation set accompanied by women in bandanas singing "longingly about Dixie" (115). Sambo and Rastus go through their act with wooden razors and dice as their props. They argue over money until a ghost suddenly appears and scares the two of them away. This the white audience finds "screamingly funny—and just like niggers" (115). The act ends with a black banjo player picking the blues; "to Sandy it seemed like the saddest music in the world—but the white people around him laughed" (116).

In LeRoi Jones's "A Poem for Willie Best" there is the same sense of comedy as a concealment of, or excuse for, horror. The poem takes the heart and life out of the comedian, leaving on display only a disembodied grin like the Cheshire Cat's. What Willie Best meant to his audience was an aggregation of stereotyped characteristics, which were funny in him, and therefore posed no threat: "Lazy / Frightened / Thieving / Very potent sexually / Scars / Generally inferior / but natural / rhythms." At the end of the poem Willie has been reduced to a "hideous mindless grin," like the one which sustained his success. This, in *Not Without Laughter,* is the piano's grin and the grin of the carnival on-lookers. In both cases laughter is a means of punishment. When Harriet is driven out of her school, the children who chase her are laughing.

All three forces, laughter, music, and Christianity, descend on Sandy in a single night. He dreams of a carnival where he hears "sad raggedy music playing while a woman shouted for Jesus in the Gospel Tent" (122). At the time when he enters the white school, these forces are inarticulate, and it is his formal education which makes them clear. Until the fifth grade he had not gone to school with white children. Stanton schools operated under a system by which in the early grades the black children were kept in separate rooms, and were taught only by black teachers. On the first day of the integrated school, the children are seated according to the alphabetical order of their names, but Sandy and the two other black children in the class are told to sit in the back. This is the first time Sandy has been told to sit apart, and he has been told this in the same context which he has also been told will make his life happy and successful.

For as long as he has lived, Sandy has been taught that education will make the difference between getting somewhere and nowhere, between freedom and dependence, and primarily between acceptability and rejection. One of Hager's great regrets is that Sandy's mother discontinued her education, while Tempy, for whom she has less affection, is nevertheless admired for having completed high school. Sandy is a "bright boy," and Hager tells him that he could become another Booker T. Washington or Frederick Douglass. She also teaches him that hate is ugly, that slavery was not so bad, that love is the essential force in the world, that white folks need black, and that therefore black folks ought not to hate white. When Hager dies, Tempy continues his education. First, she corrects his English, and teaches him to speak properly. She shifts his attention from Booker T. Washington to Du Bois, favoring the latter not for his conception of black equality but because he was an officially accomplished black man, a Harvard Ph.D. She teaches him to admire *The House Behind the Cedars*, though she respects Chesnutt's fame more than his use of dialect, and to aspire to the Talented Tenth, and become a black gentleman. She also teaches him that money buys respect.

With such encouragement and advice, Sandy decides that he does indeed wish to become a great and educated man. He quickly becomes the star pupil in his class, and dreams one night that a Christmas book Tempy had given him had turned into a chariot, and "that he was riding through the sky with Tempy standing very dignified beside him as he drove" (182). Yet, as he ponders his future, he also wonders "if he washed and washed his face and hands, he would ever be white" (183), as if the ability to become white would be the end and justification of his learning. Cleaning spitoons in the local hotel, he takes pride in the fact that his spitoons are beautiful because they are bright. He too is called bright, and as he cleans his spitoons he wonders "how people made themselves great" (226), perceiving no correspondence between himself and the object of his cleaning.

Yet gradually Sandy begins to acquire an education outside of school. This "dreamy-eyed boy who had grown to his present age largely under the dominant influence of women" (198) now enters the "men's world" through a job shining shoes in a barber shop. Kidded by the customers about his sandy-colored hair, he learns to exchange insults and play the "dozens," discovering "that so-called jokes are not really jokes at all, but rather unpleasant realities" (199). In the barber shop he also learns that Harriet has become one of Stanton's most notorious loose women, and he learns what loose women are. In his hotel job he sees a naked woman for the first time, a prostitute, and he learns that if you do not feel like dancing when a drunken Mississippi red neck tells you to, you will be fired. Later, watching his high school girlfriend turn slut in the company of a less innocent boy, he learns disappointment in love. On the Chicago streets he learns about predatory desperation.

At the end of the novel Sandy, having left Tempy and Stanton, is reunited with his mother and sister in Chicago. He has learned something about books and something about "life," and now he is headed back to school. "He's gotta be what his grandma Hager wanted him to be," says Harriet, "—able to help the black race" (323). Yet, despite the celebration and happy prospects, the ending of the book seems tacked on and unconvincing. There is a much more realistic conclusion earlier when Sandy takes a job running an elevator, just as Richard does in *Go Tell It on the Mountain* before he kills himself, because an elevator, like a formal education, is the perfect vehicle for providing the illusion of progress without the fact. As Ralph Ellison points out, it is also a vehicle for continually moving up and down between the levels of a social hierarchy.

Nothing in Sandy's past indicates that his learning or even his native intelligence will make any difference to his future. He has quietly looked about him—at Tempy, Hager, his mother and father, and Harriet—and among them all he has chosen Harriet as the ideal, because Harriet was honest with herself. Between forfeit and endurance he has chosen the latter, just as Harriet did, and in her own way, as Hager did as well. The question which Hughes leaves open is whether Sandy's endurance in pursuit of knowledge will be of any more use to him, or to "the black race," than Hager's endurance through Christianity, Harriet's endurance through music, or Jimboy's endurance through laughter. The feeling is that in education Sandy may have hit on a means of self-respect, but nobody else's.

It is a common practice in all literature, black and white, to demonstrate the penalties of learning on a sensitive and gifted child: the pain attached to a loss of innocence and increase of sophistication whereby the child's natural gifts are stunted, or the pain attached to the process of thought itself, and the accompanying discovery of the world's wickedness, or one's own. Hardy and Dickens explored this theme regularly, as did Wordsworth, Tennyson, and even

Genesis. But the treatment of the theme differs in black and white writing. In the latter the implication of conflicts involving the questionable value of education, indeed the center of the drama, is that the protagonist always had a choice. If he (Pip or Adam) had not partaken of his particular apple, and maintained his innocence, then all would have been well. But in black fiction this is not so, because there is no distinction between ignorance and innocence, and no social benefit to either. For Sandy, as for John Grimes, the option of denying his abilities seems a greater evil than attempting to fulfill them to no advantage, but the choice is really Hobson's and not his own.

Their Eyes Were Watching God

Breaking a cyclical pattern in Zora Neale Hurston's *Their Eyes Were Watching God* is not conceived of in reaction to external white forces, as it always is in Wright, for example, but rather in opposition to various forms of repression which are more generally human, and sometimes self-manufactured. The love which the heroine, Janie, eventually achieves is her means of escape, both from the restrictive considerations of practicality and from the resultant deadness in herself. Her progress in the novel, which is opposite to the progress of almost every other black character in the literature, is toward personal freedom, yet unlike McKay's Jake in *Home to Harlem* or Bita in *Banana Bottom*, whose senses of personal freedom are inborn and ready-made, Janie earns that sense the hard way. She begins as a minor character in her own life story, and ends as a full-fledged heroine whose heroism consists largely of resilience.

Born in western Florida, raised by her grandmother, Janie leads a thoroughly uneventful life until the age of sixteen. One afternoon, Janie's grandmother sees "shiftless" Johnny Taylor "lacerating her Janie with a kiss" (14). Fearful that Janie would be ruined, as Janie's mother was ruined, she pushes Janie into marriage with Logan Killicks, and his sixty acres, who looks to Janie "like some ole skull-head in de grave yard" (15), but to Nanny means security. "Tain't Logan Killicks Ah wants you to have, baby, it's protection" (17). Being a slave had made Nanny a realist about a number of things: "Honey, de white man is de ruler of everything as fur as Ah been able tuh find out. Maybe it's some place way off in de ocean where de black man is in power, but we don't know nothin' but what we see. So de white man throw down de load and tell de nigger man tuh pick it up. He pick it up because he have to, but he don't tote it. He hand it to his womenfolks" (16).

Janie marries Logan, and for a long time attempts to love him. When she finally concludes that "marriage did not make love," her "first dream was dead, so she became a woman" (25). One evening down the road comes Jody Starks, a quick-thinking, fast-talking, ambitious man, headed for a newly founded all black community, where he plans to make his fortune. Jody offers Janie a new start. Janie takes it and marries him, committing bigamy, but soon finds herself no better off than before. True to his ambition, Jody becomes mayor of the town, and the most powerful man in the area, but just as Logan had done, he begins to treat Janie like property. Finally, "something fell off the shelf inside [Janie]. Then she went inside there to see what it was. It was her image of Jody tumbled down and shattered" (63).

Their marriage disintegrates. Jody becomes ill and dies. On the morning of his death Janie studies her reflection in the mirror:

> The young girl was gone, but a handsome woman had taken her place. She tore off the kerchief from her head and let down her plentiful hair. The weight, the length, the glory was there. She took careful stock of herself, then combed her hair and tied it back up again. Then she starched and ironed her face, forming it into just what people wanted to see, and opened up the window and cried, "Come heah people! Jody is dead. Mah husband is gone from me." (75)

From that point on she performs as the respectable town widow, until her third man, Tea Cake, comes into her life. Tea Cake is a completely free spirit; each of Janie's men has successively been freer than the one before. With Tea Cake Janie finds love for the first time. Their happiness ends only when Tea Cake contracts rabies after rescuing Janie and himself from a flood. Tea Cake is driven mad by the disease and when, in delirium, he goes after Janie with a gun, she shoots and kills him in self-defense. Acquitted at her trial, Janie returns to the town where she and Tea Cake had started out, observing finally that Tea Cake "wasn't dead. He could never be dead until she herself had finished feeling and thinking. The kiss of his memory made pictures of love and light against the wall. Here was peace. She pulled in her horizon like a great fish-net. Pulled it from around the waist of the world and draped it over her shoulder. So much of life in its meshes! She called in her soul to come and see" (159).

The images of the sea which express a certain serenity at the end of *Their Eyes Were Watching God* are used to express longing, specifically Janie's, in the first lines of the book: "Ships at a distance have every man's wish on board. For some they come in with the tide. For others they sail forever on the horizon, never out of sight, never landing until the Watcher turns his eyes away in resignation, his dreams mocked to death by Time" (5). The Watcher in this instance is Janie, whose progress from states of longing to serenity in the novel seems largely accidental. Janie thinks of God as all-powerful, but disinterested, and credits the events, good and bad, of her life to an unchanging master-plan—"[God] made nature, and nature made everything else" (57). As Tea Cake is dying, Janie ponders, "Somewhere up there beyond blue ether's bosom sat He. Was He noticing what was going on around here? He must because He knew everything. Did He *mean* to do this thing to Tea Cake and her?" (146).

If it is impossible for Janie to deviate from her divine pattern, there are enough human patterns in the story available for breaking. The most binding is the prescription of her grandmother: to marry safely and well. Logan represents a sound marriage because he owns land and is therefore respectable. Jody initially appears to be a more romantic figure than Logan, but at heart is simply another, more eloquent, man of property. At a town ceremony where Jody presides over the setting up of a street lamp—"and when Ah touch de match tuh dat lamp-wick let de light penetrate inside of yuh"—a local woman bursts forth into a spiritual:

> We'll walk in de light, de beautiful light
> Come where the dew drops of mercy shine bright
> Shine all around us by day and by night
> Jesus, the light of the world. (41)

The idea, with all of its usual ramifications, is that the dark needs the light. Jody may be the leader of an all-black community, but his vision for the town, and of himself, is white, and this is the vision which Janie must shake.

Neither Jody nor Logan is depicted as being evil. What they offer is a variety of death: passionless lives lacking any sense of creativity. Silas in "Long Black Song" *(Uncle Tom's Children)* is the same kind of man. Like Logan particularly, he has worked his whole life in order to own his own house. Wright put it that "he had worked hard and saved his money and bought a farm so he could grow his own crops like white men" (120). But one day a white man, a college student, comes to his house when Silas is away, trying to sell his wife, Sarah, a combination clock and gramaphone. The white man seduces Sarah, and when Silas revenges himself, the house that he sought so long is burned to the ground with him inside of it.

The fact that Sarah allows herself to be seduced is not a sign of her promiscuity or boredom, but simply an effort at feeling human. When Silas discovers his wife's treachery, his outcry is self-condemning: "Fer ten years Ah slaved mah life out t git mah farm free" (118). For ten years and probably more, that is, he had falsified his life, trying to be successful on standard (white) terms. Even at the end, resolving to murder his white pursuers, he decides, "Ahm gonna be hard like they is!" (125). Sarah's marriage to him had been a lie, just as Janie's marriage to Logan and Jody were lies. For both women their marriages represented decisions to restrict themselves in the name of a kind of security which was white in color, and therefore unattainable.

The conflict which Janie represents, between freedom or passion and restraint or reserve, has a special quality in black fiction. The characters who deal with this conflict often seem to be carrying on the fight at a number of different levels. Gabriel Grimes's decision to become a man of God constitutes a denial or reversal of his true nature, but it also suggests an option which is significant in terms of black history. The condition of slavery was the ultimate restriction in which freedom to be oneself is out of the question. When Gabriel decides to bind his life to the straight and narrow, therefore, his decision is reactionary. As if unable to cope with his freedom, which is regarded by others as disgraceful, and by himself as perilous, he takes on the life of a slave to the church, for which he must work day and night for no pay, with no rest, and with no personal liberty in sight.

In the same way, Hager disapproves of Jimboy's singing and Harriet's dancing in implicit nostalgia for the time of her own slavery. Not that Hager would prefer slavery as an alternative to freedom, but that compared to total wildness, it seemed preferable because it was knowable. The conflict between freedom and restraint as it affects a single character is often a reflection of a particular historical situation in which freedom has been unknown for so many generations that a man would be fearful of trying it. Belonging to a people whose immediate past consisted of the freedom to serve others, it is no wonder that a character in black fiction may experience a special kind of anxiety as he contemplates being free.

As for Janie, the achievement of her freedom entails additional complications. Not only does Janie inherit the conception of the black in slavery, but of the woman in slavery as well. Remembering her grandmother's original admonition, she vents her exasperation upon Jody: "Sometimes God gits familiar wid us womenfolks too and talks His inside business. He told me how surprised He was 'bout y'all turning out so smart after Him makin' yuh different; and how surprised y'all is goin' tuh be if you ever find out you don't know half as much 'bout us as you think you do. It's so easy to make yo'self out God Almighty when you ain't got nothin' tuh strain against but women and chickens" (65). Only Tea Cake understands the source of this outburst. Because he does understand it, it is through him that Janie discovers her pride.

This discovery, the discovery of Tea Cake himself, satisfies Janie's romanticism, which has been constant throughout the novel. Such satisfaction is a rarity in this literature, and Janie's ability to fall and stay in love, even if that love is cut short, is rarer than that. Ordinarily in black fiction, love turns out to be one-sided, not because the two people involved are not equally in love with each other, but because one of them is at the same time always trying to become successful in the sense of Jody's "success" or trying in some way to deal with the white world. In *Cane* ("Theater") it is John's notion of white respectability alone which prevents him from loving Dorris, the dancer, just as it is Muriel's idea of middle class propriety which drives Dan to distraction in "Box-Seat." Florence (*Go Tell It on the Mountain*) is unable to love Frank for no other reason than that Frank is too black in color, and Rufus cannot love Leona in *Another Country* because Leona is white. In *If He Hollers Let Him Go*, Alice will only marry Bob if Bob settles down and goes to law school. In Williams' *The Man Who Cried I Am*, Lillian will only marry Max if he gives up his writing career to take a steady job. In fact, she dies aborting Max's child in order to prevent that marriage.

Their Eyes Were Watching God is structurally a simple story, yet nothing in Janie's accomplishment is simple or easy. Indeed, the enormous effort she must make in order to feel human only serves to demonstrate how strong the opposition to her humanity is. It is only when Janie and

Tea Cake marry and avoid the white world entirely that they flourish. Yet we know that Janie's achievement with Tea Cake is an unreal achievement. The two of them may escape temporarily into a fantasy of independence, but like other lovers of folklore they are aware all along that there is a world outside waiting and able to destroy them. The tragedy, and the difference, is that they have been told that the world is theirs.

Home to Harlem

The desire to discover or return to one's home is a major theme in black fiction. It has been said, probably too often, that in certain ways every American writer is continually trying to reach a home of one sort or another, but for the black writer in the twentieth century the search has had a special importance (witness the recurrence of the word "home" in a number of titles). The difficulty of feeling at home in America, combined with an ignorance of the historical home of one's people, has provided one more element behind the sense of loss and disorientation in the literature. Where characters have made an adjustment to America and stability, such as Alice's family does in *If He Hollers Let Him Go*, the sense of comfort achieved is always depicted as being illusory; whereas the true heroes of black fiction, Bigger, John Grimes, Bob Jones, the Invisible Man, and others, never have a home, real or imagined, to turn to. Whenever such characters search for one home or another, the experience is peculiarly terrifying, because they are searching not merely for something that does not exist the way they would like it to, in a dreamy sense, but for something that does not exist for them at all, a fact which they usually acknowledge at the outsets of their journeys. The act of going home ought ordinarily to be an act of rediscovery, but the paradox is that in black fiction going home becomes an effort at escape from a cycle of punishment, the idea of home itself being unknown and utopian.

The factors which contributed to the period of the

Harlem Renaissance were all connected in various ways to this home search. The sense of personal pride which Du Bois offered in opposition to the counsel of Booker T. Washington was a means of national location, of settling down. The founding of the NAACP, along with the publication of *The Crisis*, added, or attempted to add, cohesiveness. The new black writers who emerged in the twenties were bent on establishing themselves and on finding a home for their themes in the world of letters. Alain Locke, who edited *The New Negro*, declared Harlem itself the new home for art. World War I had a permanent effect on black soldiers, who were made to feel more at home in Paris than in their own army, and who, when they returned home, often found themselves isolated and out of kilter. The great migrations north were massive rejections of one homeland in pursuit of another. The era of the lost generation celebrated the feeling of homelessness generally, and made it respectable. Marcus Garvey offered a home in another country. The emergence of jazz and the blues was a way of suggesting that there might still be a home in this one.

A writer in the Harlem Renaissance approached the problem of this home search in one of two ways: either he created a blatant social protest, trying to break the color barrier by shouting directly into the faces of hatred and unfairness, or he struck out in the opposite direction, refusing to aspire to an equal life with white America, and opting instead for a primitivism which he associated with his people's roots and future well-being. The latter effort generally inspired the better literature, though there were two ways to handle the theme. One was to deal with the celebration of primitivism indirectly, through satire, as Wallace Thurman did in *The Blacker the Berry*, a satire which failed largely because it depended too much on exposition. The more effective way was Claude McKay's, whose trilogy, *Home to Harlem*, *Banjo*, and *Banana Bottom*, constituted a direct and serious confrontation with the issue, namely: if the Harlemite (black American) cannot go home to Harlem (America), where can he go?

Home to Harlem is an obvious book, and its simplicity complements the simplicity it advocates. Jake Brown returns AWOL to Harlem at the end of World War I. For a time he has tried living with a white woman in London, but now he tells the freighter which carries him, "Take me home to Harlem, Mister Ship! Take me home to the brown gals waiting for the brown boys that done show their mettle over there. Take me home, Mister Ship. Put your beak right into that water and jest move along" (9). His first night ashore, he picks up, and falls instantly in love with, a beautiful girl who asks for fifty dollars, all Jake has, to spend the night with him. In the morning the girl has returned the money and gone, and the only plot running through *Home to Harlem* is Jake's quest to retrieve her.

The bulk of this half-picaresque, half-Romantic novel consists of Jake's adventures: with a singer named Congo Rose; with his comical friend, Zeddy the Bear; a digression to Zeddy's pathetic love affair with Gin-head Susy; Jake's job as the third cook aboard a pullman car; his attachment to Ray, the intellectual; his listening to the story of Ray's life; another love affair, with Madame Laura; Ray's departure; and finally Jake's meeting again with the girl of the first night, Felice. At the end Jake takes Felice away from Zeddy, who had become Felice's escort, and Zeddy threatens to report his friend for having gone AWOL. Zeddy withdraws his threat, and the two friends are reconciled, but fearing that news of his desertion would leak out anyway, Jake and Felice decide to go to Chicago for a while. Felice says, "I hear it's a mahvelous place foh niggers" (333).

The primitivism in the novel is presented as directly as the narrative. Jake and the others are all given animal associations, which they wear gracefully: Zeddy is the Bear, and occasionally an ape; the pretentious and domineering chef on the pullman car is described as a rhino; Felice is compared to a cat; a local character named Nije is called a skunk; Billy Biase is known as The Wolf; another pullman waiter is called a mule; Jake himself is likened to a goat, and Ray, to a blue jay. As in fables, the animal associations indicate character as well as physical appearance.

They are either favorable or not, but they are never dehumanizing in the sense of suggesting the brutal. White people referred to in the novel are not known as animals. They have left the best aspects of their animalism behind them, and McKay's intimation is that their lives are therefore fake. The only characters who suffer in any way in *Home to Harlem* are Gin-head Susy and the railroad chef, both of whom pay penalties for aspiring to whiteness: Susy because she wants only light-skinned men about her, and the chef because he craves social advancement.

It is not so much that the novel derides false standards of middle-class respectability as that it revels in those things which middle-class respectability, or the standard conception of same, would find disgraceful. Not only is Jake an AWOL hero; he is not even faithful in love, taking whatever he can get until the right thing comes along again. Felice, the heroine, takes up with practically anybody until Jake returns. Zeddy's threatened treachery, the treachery of the best friend, is understood and forgiven. Indeed, everybody's social transgressions are taken in stride. Ray tells a story about a pimp named Jerco and his prostitute, Rosalind, which is a beautiful account of Jerco's valor, Rosalind's grace, and the genuine tragedy of her death. Only once in the novel is an ethical judgment made openly, when Zeddy scabs. "It ain't decent" (48), says Jake. The white man's religion is also debunked. Ray calls Jesus a bastard; Felice trusts devoutly in her magic necklace; and at one point Jake asserts, "I ain't nevah fohgitting all mah worldly goods" (20).

The most insistent aspect of primitivism in the book is the style itself. Passage after passage, *Home to Harlem* moves to the description of dancers and music, and of the ways things affect Jake's senses: "Jake and Zeddy picked two girls from a green bench and waded into the hot soup. The saxophone and drum fought over the punctuated notes. The cymbals clashed. The excitement mounted. Couples breasted each other in rhythmical abandon" (37). McKay describes the dancers at a brothel called The Baltimore:

The women, carried away by the sheer rhythm of
delight, had risen above their commercial instincts
(a common trait of Negroes in emotional states) and
abandoned themselves in pure voluptuous jazzing.
They were gorgeous animals swaying there through
the dance, punctuating it with marks of warm physical
excitement. The atmosphere was charged with
intensity and over-charged with currents of personal
reaction.   (108)

"Then," McKay writes, "five young white men unmasked
as the Vice Squad and killed the thing." Unlike the expressionism in *Not Without Laughter*, which is incidental, the
expressionism here virtually supports the action. Every
mention of color, light, and motion is elaborated upon
generously, and the novel luxuriates in these descriptions
until the reader is carried along purely by its sights and
sounds.

Technically, the reason for this dependence on the
sensuous is that the book has no other source of tension.
The only conflict in *Home to Harlem* is the classical one
of feeling versus intellect, Jake versus Ray, and it is handled
openly and gently. Ray, like his author, is West Indian and
college educated. He lives almost entirely in a cerebral
world, and marvels as much at Jake's exuberance as Jake
is astounded by Ray's sobriety. After a night on the town
together Jake asks his friend if he liked the girl he was with:

"She was kind of nice. But she had some nasty
perfume on her that turned mah stomach."
"Youse awful queer, chappie," Jake commented.
"Why, don't you ever feel those sensations that
just turn you back in on yourself and make you
isolated and helpless?"
"Wha'd y'u mean?"
"I mean if sometimes you don't feel as I felt
last night."
"Lawdy no. Young and pretty is all I feel."   (200)

Because he is an intellectual, Ray is alone in the novel. To
everybody else eroticism means freedom, and civilization,

barbarism, but, as Ray observed himself, "he was not entirely of them" (155). Depressed about his future, he acknowledges the wisdom of Jake's happier state of mind, and signs aboard a freighter as a mess boy.

There is little more to *Home to Harlem* than this: enormous pride in, and the celebration of, being black; an assertion of freedom and joy; an easy quest for happiness, achieved. Fanon exulted, "I am black: I am the incarnation of a complete fusion with the world, an intuitive understanding of the earth, an abandonment of my ego in the heart of the cosmos, and no white man, no matter how intelligent he may be, can ever understand Louis Armstrong and the music of the Congo" (*Black Skin, White Masks*, 45). This is precisely what McKay is saying with Jake, who being black, indeed named Brown, is meant to represent part of the earth itself. In many ways Jake resembles the standard natural man of American literature in general, the pioneer who discovers himself by discovering nature. He is, in this sense, the black American child of nature once removed: the uncorrupted primitive who has been snatched away from his native land, and from his own nature as well, and who now seeks to return home. Like Natty Bumppo, Jake only speaks what he feels. Like Natty, too, he confronts life with a Wordsworthian receptivity (albeit with gusto). But the essential difference is that the external nature which Jake is akin to must be guessed at. He and other characters in black fiction like him do not explore any aspect of the American wilderness because the American wilderness is not, nor has it ever been, theirs. Instead of mastering external nature in America, Jake and his people have been slaves to it, and Africa, the only natural homeland which would have any meaning to them, may only be returned to within their imaginations.

In a sense, all primitivist expressions in black fiction are variations on Rousseauistic idealism, deriving their celebrations of "the sublime and the beautiful" from the idea of color. Jake is Rousseau's man of virtue and truth, and is conceived under the assumption that man in his natural state is inherently good. If society is the corrupting agent, then man must quit society, but McKay does not believe that. What McKay seeks for his hero is the right society, a state of nature in the collective, where Jake and Ray and all the displaced people of his book can find a home in which they may practice their innate virtue. Such a society would be loosely organized, but it is a society nevertheless, and for Jake it exists neither in Harlem nor in Chicago.

This absence of home is the reality behind *Home to Harlem*, and it is the reason that the book's primitivism reaches a dead end. The novel is full of the sense of its own enthusiasm, yet it is equally filled with a sense of dread. As lost in themselves as the dancers may seem, something always threatens them, like the raid of The Baltimore. The music at Madame Laura's is described in terms of Africa:

> The piano-player had wandered off into some dim, far-away, ancestral source of music. Far, far away from music-hall syncopation and jazz, he was lost in some sensual dream of his own. No tortures, banal shrieks and agonies. Tum-tum . . . tum-tum . . . tum-tum . . . tum-tum . . . The notes were naked acute alert. Like black youth burning naked in the bush. Love in the deep heart of the jungle. . . . The sharp spring of a leopard from a leafy limb, the snarl of a jackal, green lizards in amorous play, the flight of a plumed bird, and the sudden laughter of mischievous monkeys in their green homes. (196)

Immediately afterward, Madame Laura's, like The Baltimore, is raided. The army is quietly pursuing Jake throughout the novel. The chef is instantly demoted from his high position for a single error. Ray's island nation has been taken from his people. Everyone in the novel carries weapons, which he will use. In every sensuous scene there is potential violence.

By the time McKay came to write *Banana Bottom*, he had worked out his primitivism theme completely. The heroine of *Banana Bottom*, Bita, has had an education like

Ray, but unlike Ray, who is never able to solve his inner conflicts successfully (the synthesis which he is supposed to represent in *Banjo* rings untrue), Bita is able to rise above her Western civilizing and return to her roots. Bita's last name is Plant. Returned to her native West Indies, no longer transplanted, she flourishes with an abandon unavailable to Jake and his comrades. For Jake, the permanently transplanted, home is nowhere. Trying to dissuade Ray from leaving, he says, "Why not can the idea, chappie? The sea is hell and when you hits shore it's the same life all ovah" (272). In all of the characters in *Home to Harlem* there is a vague internal native land which identifies itself in their expressions of feeling, but for each of them there is also a nation on the outside which expresses itself in terms of action. Here, as elsewhere in the literature, the incompatibility of the two areas makes home always exist in another country.

3
Exceptional
Laughter

White convention has always held that black people do a great deal of laughing, perhaps in the hope that the tag of good humor, like the tag of a sense of rhythm, might imply happiness and effect a kind of absolution. Many of America's earliest comedians were black, or in blackface, or sometimes both, and evidently it did not seem contradictory to the audiences of the Georgia Minstrels that the same people who had been forced to provide everything else for their masters should be called upon to provide hilarity as well. The use of laughter, as a demonstration of perspective, would seem to offer a perfect mechanism for allowing one's characters to escape from their particular confinement or historical cycle, yet the mechanism is rarely used in black writing. There are good-humored characters in the literature such as Jimboy in *Not Without Laughter* and Tea Cake in *Their Eyes Were Watching God*; malevolently humorous characters such as The Weasel in *Country Place*; a few witty ironists such as Bob Jones of *If He Hollers Let Him Go*; clowns such as McKay's Zeddy the Bear (*Home to Harlem*) who are funny unintentionally; and there are pitchmen and tricksters such as William Kelley's Cooley (*dem*), Cecil Brown's George Washington (*The Life and Loves of Mr. Jiveass Nigger*), and Ellison's Rinehart (*Invisible Man*). With a few exceptions, however, black fiction has failed to produce the full, self-sustaining humorous hero, primarily because humor is out of place in what is basically a tragic literature.

Because the literature is basically tragic, whatever humor occurs in it takes on a special purpose. More than providing the conventional "relief" from a tragic circumstance, humor in black fiction serves as an instrument of perception, as a way of looking critically at a reality which is not funny. The seriousness of the reality is in fact made clearer by a humorous perspective. Yet humor does not improve that reality by its existence, nor, even in satire, suggest that such improvement is possible. For the characters who use it, it is a way of surviving within, not beating, the cyclical system, which is why the few wholly humorous characters who have existed in black fiction have achieved a brand of universality at once unique and credible.

The achievement of universality in black literature is particularly remarkable, more so than in modern literature generally, because it depends on hard data. The commonly recognized everyman of the modern novel is so called because he shows himself to be confused and powerless in the age of Freud and machines, and is therefore punished and abused by abstract phenomena. Whatever his predicament, he usually comes out of it and gains a certain strength by acknowledging that his lot is ordinarily human, that when he faces himself squarely, he is like all men and women, all of whom share the same joys, griefs, frustrations, and so forth. In fact, he comes very close to the everyman of the *Pilgrim's Progress*. Tempted, guileless, and rueful, he earns his universality as an innocent in an allegory.

Few black heroes are "universal" in this way. There are enough hard facts of life common to American black culture to make allegory unnecessary. The existence of these common experiences allows an author not only to anticipate more set assumptions on the part of the reader, but to free his major character from a passive role. To one degree or another, the black everyman is every black man. Because a writer can take that as a given, no black hero has to start his pilgrimage from scratch. The personified vices and virtues which beset the man can be refined into individuals, and the hero in turn can be more wary and resourceful in his dealings with them.

This is to say, in effect, that there is no such thing as an everyman in black fiction, either in the modern or ancient sense. Instead, the expectation of circumscribed patterns creates an "everyworld" in which individual characters play up their idiosyncrasies, and leave the moral lessons to be culled from plots and themes. Yet there are characters in the literature who are called "everyman," and these, interestingly, are the humorists. They become everyman in the exact opposite mold of Christian. Their universality derives from their being able to deal cannily with the universe, which not only makes them exceptional in black fiction, but ideal as modern heroes.

The "Simple" Collections

The most famous humorous character in black fiction is Langston Hughes's Jesse B. Semple, called Simple. Simple is not a true exception to the cyclical patterns of the fiction because he never operates within a fully developed and cohesive plot; therefore, unlike the hero of a novel, or even a short story, he is not responsible for sustaining his character over a distance. Nevertheless, he is unique among black fictional characters in that he survives his stories with a sense of pride. Indeed, he is one of the few characters in the literature who survive at all. He does not break a cyclical pattern because Hughes does not make his life available to it, but as a social commentator, he observes the various patterns, and as a humorist, depends upon their existence.

Modeled on a factory worker Hughes met in a Harlem bar in the early forties, Simple became known as the "Negro Everyman," and during the twenty years of his prominence his commentary filled over a hundred and fifty columns of the *Chicago Defender* and the *New York Post*, five books, and a Broadway musical. He was the embodiment of an ideal intelligence, at once shrewd, generous, irreverent, resilient, contemptuous of hypocrisy, inconsistent, manly, unrefined, and sane. He held opinions on everything which were rarely encumbered with facts, and he had little formal learning. In the Simple sketches Hughes pits his own college education against Simple's native sense, and as is always the case in such literary battles, the college education comes in second. The name, Jesse B. Semple, was a combination of advice and imperative, and in his so-called simplicity, Simple joined the corps of American folk hero humorists—Uncle Remus, Josh Billings, Mr. Dooley, and others—who drew laughter out of the shock and novelty of common sense. Simple may not always have been as funny as his predecessors, but he was a richer character and much more complicated.

He was an urban folk hero, equipped with city tastes and a city vocabulary, yet he was as ardent a regionalist as Sam Slick, Jonathan Oldstyle, Hosea Biglow, or any of the rural American humorists. It made no difference that Simple's region was Harlem and that his dialect was Harlem argot; his attitude toward his section of the country was as elaborately loyal as a Westerner's or Down-Easter's, and he was just as purely a home-grown philosopher. He was brash, as are all literary regionalists, he was anti-authoritarian, and in spite of his critical stance and occasional doomsday visions, he was an optimist at heart. Where he differs from his fellow regionalists is that his region was continually under attack, because in a larger sense than Harlem his region was blackness; and so the criticisms he leveled at the nation were often informed by a sense of urgency and frustration which, until the emergence of contemporary black comedians such as Dick Gregory and Godfrey Cambridge, was unique in American humor. There was also the difference between a cracker barrel and a bar stool. The fact that Simple did his philosophizing from a local dive was designed to be one of his comic properties, but it also suggested that in order to sustain his hopeful view of the world it helped to be high, if only on beer.

Above everything, he was a race man: "'you certainly are race-conscious,' I said. 'Negroes, Negroes, Negroes! Everything in terms of race. Can't you think just once without thinking in terms of color?' 'I am colored,' said Simple" (*Simple Takes a Wife*, 22). In an essay on feet ("Feet Live Their Own Life," *Simple Speaks His Mind*, henceforth abbreviated *Mind*, 3) he lists the places where his feet have stood—at lunch counters, WPA desks, hospitals, graves, welfare windows, craps tables, kitchen doors, social security railings, soup lines, and the draft—all of which make up the Harlemite's itinerary. When his companion asks if there is anything truly special about his feet, he tells of a night in a Harlem street riot when one of his feet was used to kick in a store window, while the other was getting set to make a run for it. Inside the playfulness there is terror and indignation, yet the playfulness prevails. He composes poems about Jim Crow, feels the beating of Emmet Till as if it were happening to himself, and still can joke about a Second Coming in which Jesus gets rid of all white people except for Mrs. Roosevelt. He can also poke fun at his own, mocking the kinds of articles that characterized black magazines of the fifties, and vowing that if he were in charge of one of such rags he would put out a three-part series, the first installment to be called *Can Sex Pass*, the second *Sex Seized in Passing*, the third *Please Pass the Sex*. Simple could make his readers feel angry, giddy, and abashed simultaneously, and remain totally invulnerable to their feelings, like a good magician. His carapace was his honesty, not his humor, and when he said something like "I am colored," one smiled, not because the statement was funny, but because it was sublimely true.

This sense of the sublime in him, rather than his own sense of the ridiculous, accounts for Simple's effect. The laughter his pieces inspire springs from two antithetical impulses. One is the classical state of our feeling superior to him, not because he is silly or duped—he is rarely duped —but because he has been through a mill that most of his readers are safe from, at least at the moment of reading. Yet the other side of our laughter comes from sheer admiration and wonderment, out of our recognition that Simple is thoroughly superior to the things which have declared his inferiority. He is endurance itself. In his time, he boasts, he has been "laid off, fired, and not rehired, Jim Crowed, segregated, insulted, eliminated, locked in, locked out, locked up, left holding the bag, and denied relief . . . but I am still here" ("Census," *Simple's Uncle Sam*, henceforth abbreviated *Sam*, 1). Throughout the sketches he repeats "I am still here" as if in defiance of a roll call which expected silence at his name. In a way, his humor derives from our perception that his obstinate desire to survive and flourish in the face of overwhelming odds is an absurd consistency, endurance being his humor in the Jonsonian sense. Yet we laugh more at the magnificence of the consistency than at its foolishness, as we would at the sight of something stunningful beautiful.

To create a character whom we simultaneously laugh up to and down on takes an acute sense of balance. Hughes's method in the sketches was the standard one of setting up conversations between Simple and his friend, Boyd, which would serve as springboards for Simple's opinions and flights of imagination; but Hughes deviated from the pattern by giving Boyd a developed personality and a personal history. Ben Franklin's Silence Dogood, Seba Smith's Jack Downing, and other such characters who used the gimmick of letters addressed either to editors or imaginary relatives merely implied the existence of a third-party listener when they were confronting the reader directly. George W. Harris used an actual narrator for Sut Lovingood, but only as a kind of cattle prod, injecting "who"s and "why"s into Sut's monologues the way that Edgar Bergen would set up Charlie McCarthy for the punch lines. Mark Twain used a narrator in "The Celebrated Jumping Frog of Calaveras County" who, like Boyd, was more of a gentleman than the main attraction; but Twain's speaker was only a straight man, created to heighten the humor by incongruity. Mr. Dooley had his Hennessy, but Hennessy functioned solely as an interviewer who was no more educated, and a good deal duller, than his friend. In contrast to these Boyd is a lively, intelligent, likeable, and completely believable man. Simple trusts and admires him, and is responsible for our doing the same.

Occasionally, as in "Lynn Clarisse" (*Sam*, 83), where Boyd is trying to pick up Simple's cousin, Hughes lets his narrator out on his own, but he cannot afford to do this often for fear of dividing the reader's attention. Because Simple is the wiser and more clever of the two it is essential that he dominate the sketches, yet Simple would not be half so effective a critic without his companion's presence. Susanne Langer points out (in *Feeling and Form*) that we tend to laugh at things in the theater which we might not think funny in life because we are not laughing at what the jokes mean to us, but what they mean to the play. There is a kind of two-man play being performed in all the Simple pieces, a play that progresses nowhere, has no beginning, middle, and end, but that nevertheless contains a number of distinguishable players (albeit most of them offstage), a distinct setting, a major character, a minor character, and a series of scenes. If, when we laugh at Simple's humor, we are merely laughing at the exercise of a comic spirit within a theatrical (unreal) framework, then none of Simple's social commentary can be too painful or outrageous. But neither can it be meaningful or effective. This is clearly one reason for minimizing Boyd's time "on stage," to avoid diminishing Simple's prominence and therefore increasing the power of his direct address to the reader.

But there is also a special sense of timing in operation here. Simple rarely starts any of his protest pieces with a protest. Usually he begins griping about something inane and irrelevant, and then only after a while does he strike his theme. He strings his reader along in an obvious and expectable way; but the real trick is Hughes's, because by allowing just enough dialogue to go on between Simple and Boyd before the protest theme is reached he lets his reader think he is watching a play throughout. We laugh, then, at what the humor means to the play, and we continue to laugh long after the play construction has been dropped, after Boyd has dropped out, and right on into Simple's speech (on segregation, personal ethics, or national brutality), which is not spoken to any character but to ourselves. If we do not laugh outright, we are at least pleased, and it is no easy feat to please people in their own instruction.

Like every comic realist, Simple is at heart a dreamer. Boyd, who is much more of a realist, takes him up on this fact often, and Simple admits it freely. There is a connection in his mind between dreaming and optimism, yet his comic fantasies are usually ominous and baleful. His sense of the fantastic is the satirist's sense. Commenting obliquely on black people as invisible men, he envisions a demonstration in which every black in the country, including Martin King, Adam Powell, "every waitress in Chock Full o' Nuts," and the Black Muslims, would take off his clothes so that "America would be forced to scrutinize our cause" ("Pose-Outs," *Sam*, 109). In another piece he worries that as yet there are no Negro astronauts in space, "because if one of them white Southerners gets to the moon first, 'Colored Not Admitted' signs will go up all over heaven as sure as God made little green apples, and Dixiecrats will be asking the man in the moon, 'Do you want your daughter to marry a Nigra?'" ("The Moon," *Sam*, 28). His gazes into the future foresee exaggerations of the present by which the present is itself held up to ridicule. What he accomplishes with them is a projection of logical consequence, as if to say that if you doubt the craziness of the world we have now, let me show you how it will look done to a turn. Despite his fantasies, however, Simple can be as practical as Boyd. When his friend asks him if he would be the first to volunteer for the black "nude-out," Simple answers, "That honor I would leave to you."

The other device that Hughes puts to use is dialect, and Simple handles the device in a conventional way. Hughes did not indulge in the practice, which one often sees elsewhere, of misspelling words that his character pronounces correctly (for example, *luv*), and therefore making it appear as if the character is an illiterate writing the sketch rather than a speaking participant in it. Simple, however, does misplace *s*'s, add *-ations*, say "do" for "does," make verbs out of nouns, and generally mispronounce what is formally considered to be correct English. Such defects of language are traditionally supposed to be comic because they make the reader feel that he possesses a higher culture and more education than the speaker. This is a particular trap for the portion of the white audience that—beneath the condescension it took to be amused by the sketches in the first place—believes all blacks to be ignorant and wants them to sound like it. One of the things that made Amos and Andy's Kingfish, Rochester of the

Jack Benny program, and Mantan Moreland and Willie Best of the movies so hilarious to white audiences was the way they spoke. Accordingly, dialect was a peculiarly touchy device for Hughes to employ because he knew that his black readers would resent anything that smacked of stereotype. (In "Summer Ain't Simple" he criticizes certain white representations of black life by having Simple observe that his papa wasn't rich, and his mama wasn't good looking.) What Hughes did with dialect was what Twain had done with Huck, and Henry Shaw had done with Josh Billings; he made it an integral part of his hero's intelligence. The mistakes of diction which Simple makes are subsumed in that intelligence, are neutralized by it, and indeed are transformed. Not only does Simple dignify dialect, he makes the King's English seem awkward in comparison.

The use of dialect raises the question of whether Simple's audiences of black and white readers are distinct and show distinguishable responses. Such a speculation would not apply to "serious" black writing, either poetry or fiction, because in those cases we assume that the writer writes for an inner audience which is largely colorblind. In *Native Son*, for example, Wright may have considered the effects of his story on white and black readers separately, hoping for different kinds of awakening in each, but one still feels that such consideration was secondary to the professional and private exercise of his craft. With Hughes, however, the question of audience becomes more pertinent because in writing humor one must always theoretically be facing outward in order to court the laughter which is the only sort of approbation available. Simple is a black man, not making fun of black life, yet making fun out of it. When a white man laughs at this fun, is it the guilty laugh, the sympathetic laugh, Beckett's "dianoetic" laugh (*Watt*), or is it punitive? When the black man laughs, is it nervousness, embarrassment, revenge, or magnanimity?

At one point in the "Census" sketch Simple complains that, because the census taker was white, he did not understand when Simple was making a joke. It is not true that white readers do not understand when Simple is joking, but the problem is what they understand those jokes to mean. A black reader may laugh at "Feet" because of self-pity, or because he is a secret sharer. For the white reader the reasons may be similar, but they can never be the same, and it is more likely that he laughs out of shame than anything else. The black reader too may feel shame, but it is the shame of what has happened to him, not at what he has caused to happen. Yet it also may be that no group feeling is present at all.

Bergson believed that the act of laughter suggests a complicity with other laughers, but in reading Simple it is questionable whether such complicity is felt. It seems more often than not that Simple is addressing the private best in our black or white selves, which we always believe to be in opposition to the public (or group) worst. Whenever he indicates that the nation is made up of fools, we read "the rest of the nation." He often does not appeal to fellow feeling in his readers as much as he does to the personal and isolated situation and, in a sense, to individual vanity, which is an educable element. Moreover, whether or not there is a color line in his audience, Simple does not seem to care in the least who his readers are or what they think. With most humorists, literary or real, we always get the sense of how fragile they are, that after three consecutive jokes without raising a chuckle they would disintegrate. But Simple seems entirely careless of our appraisal. He may appeal to our vanity, but he sustains himself on pride.

In *The Book of Negro Humor*, which Hughes edited, Roi Ottley records an anecdote about Robert S. Abbott, the founder and editor of the *Chicago Defender*. A judge named Abernathy in a small Georgia town was running for re-election on a Jim Crow platform. Blacks in the town sent Abernathy's campaign literature to Abbott, who instructed his staff to pillory Abernathy in an editorial. Abbott then sent five hundred copies of the editorial back to Abernathy's town for distribution, but when Abernathy's opponent reprinted the editorial for one of his own pamphlets, and acknowledged the source, Abernathy was re-elected by a landslide. The would-be heroes of the story, Abbott and the *Defender* staff, are hoist with their own petard, a classically comic circumstance. The unexpected occurs, Abernathy turns the tables on his enemies, and as in cartoons where the chased outwits the chasers, the audience is supposed to laugh at the triumph of a lucky scoundrel. Yet, all the humor in the anecdote derives from hatred: the judge's hatred of blacks, the town's hatred of blacks and their Northern newspaper, Abbott's hatred of Abernathy, and our own hatred of hatred as well. What we are laughing (or more likely smiling) at is only partly the irony of the judge's good fortune. That is a reflex laugh, the situation demands it. But we are laughing primarily at our disappointment in humanity generally, and in ourselves. The anecdote is a pathetic story. It is funny largely because of its pathos, which we appreciate because of our confidence in the inevitable perseverance of human idiocy. In a sense our reaction defies the Bergsonian rule, because instead of laughing at the unexpected in the tale, we laugh at the all too readily expected. But the all too readily expected can be as much of an aberration as total surprise. Given enough time even the consistency of bigotry becomes laughable.

Nobody understood this phenomenon more fully than Hughes, who continually drew laughter from the unlaughable. Hazlitt ("On Wit and Humour") said that humor makes the ludicrous lead us to the pathetic, and in his choice of subject matter this is precisely what Simple does. He jokes about poll taxes, segregation, governmental corruption and neglect, disenfranchisement, unemployment, hunger, ignorance, ghetto living conditions, the Ku Klux Klan, in short, about everything that is inherently unfunny. Hughes himself said that "humor is what you wish in your heart were not funny" (*The Book of Negro Humor*, vii). To Simple there is nothing so terrible in the world that it cannot be made to seem ridiculous. He is purely and unrelentingly a social critic. As Benchley took his humor from the upper reaches of the middle class, from the perils of tennis games and hotel suites, Simple took his from the harassment of his people and the continuation of their servitude. Surprisingly for a literary figure, he only rarely deals in literary jokes—in "Matter for a Book" (*Mind*), he wants to follow on Frank Yerby's success with *The Foxes of Harrow* by writing *The Wolves of Harlem*—and even more rarely is he witty or ironic. Nor will he indulge in savage or cruel comedy; the episode of the street riot is a joke about escape, not destruction. What he cares about exclusively are the troubles of being black, and he makes laughter out of his own mistreatment.

Yet, along with being an ordinary man of his people, Simple has an evangelical strain, a strain which is evident in the low-key preaching he does, and in the structure of the sketches themselves. Each of these pieces is built as a sermon. Not all of them deal with references to religion, though many do; but every one of them is modeled on the revivalist pattern of the preacher making an opening statement, which is followed by a pause in which the congregation says "amen" or an equivalent, which is in turn followed by the preacher's expansion of the topic at hand using examples drawn usually from his own experience. The use of this structure for comic rather than devotional purposes has been part of American stand-up comedians' routines for a long time. When Red Buttons began his act with "Strange things are happening," or when Rodney Dangerfield starts out with "Nobody gives me any respect," the idea was, and is, for the audience to think "amen," and then gear itself for the jokes to follow. Twain said that he was always preaching when he wrote, that if the humor emerged as part of the sermons, fine, but that he would have written the sermons in any case. We get something of this feeling with Simple. His sermons are part of himself and so they are humorous naturally, but because like Twain he is first a moral man, then a humorist, we realize that amusement is not the most important reaction intended.

There is a complication, however, in Simple's use of the religious framework which would probably not exist if he were white. Whenever he makes jokes or fantasizes about heaven or angels or God, he is working within the convention of gently irreverent, folksy, and familiar humor, the kind that *Green Pastures* is made of. The main difference is tone, and Simple's tone, like the tone on this subject throughout black fiction generally, is affected by his suspicion that he may be joking about someone else's God, a white one. There is a sketch called "God's Other Side" *(Sam)* in which Simple says that he would prefer to sit at the left hand of God instead of the right, like everyone else, so as to get more attention; but lighthearted as this piece is, underlying it there is the intimation that Simple and all blacks must always pay court to God's other side. In "Empty Houses" he recalls wondering if the white Jesus he had learned to pray to as a child "cared anything about a little colored boy's prayers" *(Sam, 15)*. In all the sketches the religious joking lacks confidence, and without confidence the jokes develop an edge. Similarly his religious satires can sound heavyhanded, as is the case with "Cracker Prayer" *(Sam)*, which when compared to something as finely controlled as John Betjeman's "In Westminster Abbey" seems ominous and seething.

As *Native Son, Go Tell It on the Mountain, Cane,* and many other novels suggest, no single aspect of black life in America has affected black literature as deeply as religion. In *Another Country* Ida, who is bent on revenge against the white world, remarks that she "learned all [her] Christianity from white folks" (237). She speaks bitterly because the God acquired was a God imposed, and along with the acquisition came a thousand crimes committed in His name. There is no major black author who has not grappled with the ambiguity of trying to believe in a religion which was used as a mollifying instrument for slaves, which promises future salvation while contributing to present isolation and torment, and which may, for all its promises, contain a heaven for whites only and be a hoax. This is the background to Simple's religious humor. When he speaks of St. Peter and the Pearly Gates it is not the voice of a man who trusts what he is making fun of, but of a man who is making a joke of something because he is supposed to trust it, yet does not. By poking fun at heaven Simple is partly poking fun at himself and all other black people for whom heaven may be unattainable. There is fear behind this humor, but there is safety too; for if heaven and God do not exist for him after all, laughter may create the perspective to anticipate the loss.

The most remarkable thing about Simple is that he can be edgy or shaky in his humor or opinions, he can be grumpy or sour, digressive, illogical, wrong-headed, he can even be dull without losing our affection or attention or anything in himself. There is so much fluidity and grace in his make-up that he always seems larger than the sum total of his effects and defects as well. At the end of a piece called "Dog Days" he simply runs out of ideas, but instead of stopping neatly he suddenly switches the topic from dogs to a dogwood tree and a girl whom he once kissed under it. When the consecutive-minded Boyd asks, "Why did you bring that up?" Simple says, "To revive my remembrance" (Sam, 106). The feat of these touches is that they regularly remind us that Simple is more of a human being than a pundit. In this he comes much closer to a folk hero like Davy Crockett than to a closet wit such as Jonathan Oldstyle, because he has a life apart and distinguishable from his sense of humor. If one were to imagine an instance when Mr. Dooley were publicly proven wrong in his judgment of an important issue, it is likely that Mr. Dooley's reputation would suffer because his whole being relies on the accuracy of his wit. This is not the case with Simple. He is more interesting than his intelligence, and he outlives it. Nothing can shake him, no mishap and no mistake.

He is, first of all, a completely honest man, about himself particularly; and because his brand of honesty is so scarce it becomes one of his comic attributes. As deeply as he is committed to the causes of civil rights, it is not an ethereal subject with him, and he shows nothing but melancholy derision for senseless martyrdom. In "Swinging High" he comments upon the death of a white Cleveland minister who, as part of a protest against racial discrimination, lay down behind a bulldozer: "I gather there are some things you would not do for a cause," said Boyd. "I would not lay down behind a bulldozer going backwards" (*Sam*, 7), said Simple. His candor also extends to the way he makes his points, loosely and without apparent premeditation. The sketch on "Bomb Shelters" (*Sam*) deals with the inanity of planning shelters for a Harlem tenement whose quarters are so cramped that the shelters would not be able to accommodate all the tenants, and which is probably about to collapse anyway. Simple imagines a situation in which he is battling his neighbors to get inside the shelter, a notion which undoubtedly would have appealed to James Thurber. But what Thurber would have done with it would have been to invent a fable in which would be exhibited all the selfishness people, or animals, are capable of, selfishness akin to the evil that creates the necessity of bomb shelters in the first place. Simple's style, on the other hand, is to avoid the moral. He builds his theme haphazardly, letting the laughs arise where they may, creating a full scene. By this he suggests that nothing is funny or sad in isolation, himself included.

The honesty Simple uses to aid his humor works for other effects as well. When he feels prejudiced, he says so directly. When he feels sanctimonious or sentimental he is equally open. He gets away with total candor because he is recognizably a good man, good enough even to laugh at his own virtue: "Now me, my specialty is to walk on water" ("Soul Food," *Sam*, 111). His goodness is intimately bound to his simplicity—which, at its conventional level, merely takes the shape of wanting to strip the frills from things, of disliking high tone and preferring soul food to French cooking, natural hairdos to wigs, gospel to Italian opera, the Apollo Theater to the Met, and so on. But in a more fundamental way Simple's simplicity represents his effort to discover who he is and where he has come from. It is the classic circumstance in black literature of the hero's search for roots. By giving Simple his name Hughes implies that for a black man to be simple is a most difficult achievement. It means holding on to a sense of self and manhood in a strange land that conspires daily against one's doing so.

In the piece "Concernment" Simple and Boyd have a rare squaring off, triggered when Boyd gets bogged down trying to remember the exact word in a quotation. Simple says, "Boyd your diploma is worth every penny you paid for it. Only a man who is colleged could talk like that. Me, I speaks simpler myself" (Sam, 152). Boyd counters by observing that sometimes simplicity can be more devious than erudition, to which Simple answers, "Of course." As usual Simple gets the last word, but by agreeing with Boyd he also makes a point. The reason Simple maintains his simplicity is not because he cannot fathom complications. Indeed, he gives the impression that he has already been through the complications of a subject and that these have allowed him finally to arrive at his simple conclusion. What comes through instead of a contempt for complexities is a weariness of talking about them. The kind of maxim Simple coins is "Greater love hath no man than that he lay down his life to get even" ("Junkies," Sam, 98). The kind of wisdom he lives by is that "there is no way for a man to commit bigamy without being married" ("Simple on Women," Book of Negro Humor, 146). If there are exceptions to his rules he takes them up one by one, but he refuses to be caught with an all-encompassing thesis on anything because such things carry a complacency which is alien to his nature and also impose a rigidity of their own.

Unlike the pseudo-innocent boy observers of American humor, Simple is a full-fledged grown-up. He has been married and separated, is seeking and eventually obtains a divorce (which on principle he refuses to pay for), is courting one respectable woman while having an occasional fling with another less respectable one, has been, as he says, "cut, stabbed, run over, hit by a car, tromped by a horse, robbed, fooled, deceived, double-crossed, dealt seconds" ("Census," Sam, 2), can hold his liquor, believes very little he hears, and is beginning to go gray. As an adult he is not burdened by demands that his behavior or thinking be consistent. In separate sketches he toasts Harlem as paradise and condemns it as hell. He deplores warfare, composes a beautiful prayer against it, but admits, "I would not mind a war if I could win it" ("A Toast to Harlem," *Mind*, 34). On the race issue he can, in different moods, sound contemplative or belligerent. He lives most of his time in a dream world and yet values nothing as highly as money and possessions. Having no use for education himself, he nevertheless would establish a fund to send all the young people in Harlem to college. He is a confirmed capitalist, yet fantasizes about the coming of a socialist millennium. At one point he brags to Boyd, "I am the toughest Negro God's got" ("Family Tree," *Mind*, 26). In a quieter spirit he confesses that he drinks because "I'm lonesome inside myself" ("Conversation on the Corner," *Mind*, 20).

There is a moment in the movie *Humoresque* when Oscar Levant turns to John Garfield and says, "Don't blame me, I didn't make the world; I barely live on it." The sense Simple gives us is just that: of a man who can take anything, who can roll with the punches, bounce back, punch back if aroused, and at the same time who seems to be living on a better and cleaner plane than the world he contends with. In his "Character Notes" to the play *Simply Heavenly*, Hughes aptly describes Simple as Chaplinesque. Like Chaplin, Simple was the complete humorous creation. There has never been a character in black literature like him, nor is there likely to be another one in the future. For all his combativeness Simple was a standard American dreamer who believed in progress within the system, and his optimism would have been incompatible with the present-day mood. Moreover, in a time of real and verbal militancy humor is judged to be a harmful distraction, or "counterproductive." Yet he could not have been born in a period earlier than he was, either—not in the late twenties and early thirties when black writers were bent on producing serious books and establishing the Harlem Renaissance, and certainly not before then, when whatever black writing existed was done by apologists. Simple came, flourished, and went at just the right time. Even a few years before Hughes's death in 1967 he was beginning to sound a little out of things, a little forced.

Everyone knows that humorists perish rapidly, that unlike tragedy, which endures from age to age, humor generally thrives only within the lifetime of a particular taste. If Simple turns out to be the exception to this rule it will not be because the jokes he made held their flavor, but because the image of man he represented was important to hold on to. On the level of vital statistics no one could have stood further from the packaged ideal of American heroism. He was disqualified from this designation by his loose love life, his upbringing, his habits, his age, his physique, his disrespectful attitude, his friends, his absence of prospects, and especially his color. Yet from a no less idealistic viewpoint Simple was more the embodiment of the all-American boy than a dozen Frank Merriwells or Jack Armstrongs. He was the fighter who knew when to quit, the resourceful, canny mind which could wax poetic on an impulse, the man unencumbered by possessions, the free man, the generous Joseph, the stumbler who admitted his mistakes, the surviver and the dreamer. To Schiller the aim of comedy was a liberation from all violence, cruelty, and stupidity. If Simple was more skeptical about such liberation being man's destiny, at least he felt it was worth a try. For himself he sought nothing but human decency between the races. When so simple a wish was persistently denied, he had to laugh.

Manchild in the Promised Land

In many ways Claude Brown's Sonny of *Manchild in the Promised Land* is Simple updated and enclosed in a single narrative. Sonny's humor is tougher than Simple's, and because of its context, more sporadic and occasional, but it has the same essential force of Simple's humor, tackles the same subject matter, depends on the same candid lack of innocence, and is inspired by the same transparent didacticism. Sonny is the "Negro Everyman" on an organized pilgrimage. When his story begins he is already supposed to be located in the promised land, but because the promises of his particular land have been broken, the point of his pilgrimage is to make an escape. He succeeds because, like Simple, he is able to create laughter where none is expected, and in a sense, to transport himself to safety by means of his own perspective.

Sonny is growing up in Harlem in the 1950's. At the beginning of the story he is caught during a robbery, shot in the stomach, and is awaiting detention in the New York State Training School for Boys. "Mama tried to change the judge's mind by telling him that I had already been to Wiltwyck School for Boys for two and a half years. And before that, I had been ordered out of the state for at least one year. She said that I had been away from my family too much; that was why I was always getting into trouble" (16). The novel proceeds to shuffle among anecdotes, going back to Sonny's neighborhood, his education in the streets, and the time he spent at the Wiltwyck School. The first half of the book ends when he is released from the Training School, and returns to a changed Harlem.

The lessons he took in pranks as a child now, in his teens, become lessons in crime. Drugs have hit Harlem, and one by one Sonny watches the friends of his youth turn addict, prostitute, and pusher. Sonny begins to want out. He takes a number of jobs, and enrolls in high school. He continues to serve as a spectator on the street scene, but gradually begins to live independently, playing the piano in a group, experimenting with religion, eventually falling in love with a Jewish girl whose parents reject him. His deepest worry is his kid brother, Pimp, whom he suspects is on drugs. At the end, Pimp is lost to drugs, old friends are dead or transformed, yet Sonny has achieved the strength to move on.

He has grown up in the promised land, and the allusions to Exodus and the Old Testament generally are manifold. The emergence of heroin is conceived of as "a plague, and the plague usually afflicted the eldest child of every family, like the one of the firstborn with Pharaoh's people in the Bible. Sometimes it was even worse than the biblical plague" (188). Harlem has its "neighborhood prophets" as well, and its judges: "You givin' us the same chance we had before" (123). And Sonny has his various parables, on which he depends for practical guidance:

> Well, there were two frogs sitting on a milk vat
> one time. The frogs fell into the milk vat. It was very
> deep. They kept swimming and swimming around, and
> they couldn't get out. They couldn't climb out because
> they were too far down. One frog said, "Oh, I can't
> make it, and I'm going to give up." And the other frog
> kept swimming and swimming. His arms became more
> and more tired, and it was harder and harder and
> harder for him to swim. Then he couldn't do another
> stroke. He couldn't throw one more arm into the milk.
> He kept trying and trying; it seemed as if the milk
> was getting hard and heavy. He kept trying; he knows
> that he's going to die, but as long as he's got this little
> bit of life in him, he's going to keep on swimming.
> On his last stroke, it seemed as though he had to pull
> a whole ocean back, but he did it and found himself
> sitting on top of a vat of butter.   (128)

Sonny's father, whom he fears, plays the shell game with him, and provides a different parable: "After I made the last wrong pick, Dad looked at me and just kept shaking his head for a little while. Then he said, 'That's jis what you been doin' all your life, lookin' for a pea that ain't there' " (73). When Sonny sees Pimp on drugs, he thinks, "Absalom, Absalom" (311).

The Old Testament allusions and devices go deeply into *Manchild in the Promised Land*, touching upon the shared experiences of the black man and the Jew, the mutual identification, and often the mutual hatred. Other novels and stories in black fiction brush this topic briefly, as in the Jewish-Communist associations in *Native Son* and *If He Hollers Let Him Go* and the cultural antagonism set up in James McPherson's "A Matter of Vocabulary," but here the situation is laid open. Brown begins with a half-joke of a definition:

"They got crackers down there, ain't they, Sonny?"
"Yeah, Mama said they got crackers down South."
"Sonny, what is crackers? They ain't the kinda
crackers you buy in the candy store, is they?"
"No, the crackers down South is white people,
real mean white people."
"Is Mr. Goldman a cracker, Sonny?"
"No, he's a Jew."
"But he's white and look real mean."
"I know that, but some white people is crackers
and some a dem is Jews, and Mr. Goldman is a Jew.
You see, Pimp, white people is all mean and stingy. If
one-a dem is more stingy than he is mean, he's a Jew;
and if he is more mean than he is stingy, then he's
a cracker." (44)

Brown moves from side to side in Sonny's opinions, from
Sonny's respect for and dependence on the Meitners and
the Cohens, who coach and encourage him, and his admiration for what he judges to be the common sense of Jews—
"They have their synagogues; they have their bakerys, their
grocery stores. Man, those people aren't easily bullshitted"
(333)—to his contempt for Goldberg, who called a sixty-
year-old black housekeeper "girl," and his disgust about
prejudice in Jews: "This was the relationship between the
Jew and the descendents of Ham. We were all right. We
were supposed to work for them; we were good enough for
this, good enough to clean their houses. They were supposed to sympathize with us. I think sometimes the sympathy used to bother me more than anything else, this
attempt at being liberal-minded" (299).
     The question of how Sonny is going to think about
Jews remains unresolved as long as he thinks categorically.
The heart of the conflict, as he acknowledges, is that the
Jew and the black man, when opposed to each other, contend that each should know better. Baldwin once noted that
anti-Semitism is part of the American scene, and that a certain amount of black anti-Semitism stems from the cultural
desire to be acceptable. Brown cites this phenomenon—
"The people would holler, 'Yeah! Yeah! Them goddam

Jews killed my Jesus too' " (348)—but Sonny leaves that thinking to the mob. Eventually he confronts the problem personally in his love affair with the Jewish girl whom he meets in school, and when her parents destroy their relationship out of bigotry, Sonny, not really wiser on the large historical question of Jews and blacks, at least has dealt with the question in terms of individuals.

Manchild in the Promised Land is about individuals, specifically Sonny, yet it also sits squarely within three prominent American literary traditions: American folk humor, the American success story, and the American Gothic, the tale of horror. As folk humor it is a miniature classic. Like Simple, Sonny takes on the characteristics of the Yankee peddler, the man of all trades and disguises, and of the confidence man as well. In a false conversion scene, one repeated incidentally in the autobiographies of Hughes and Wright, he seeks to prove that he has seen the light in order to make an impression on June Rogers, the daughter of Mrs. Rogers, the powerhouse of the church: "I started clapping my hands and jumping up and down and saying, 'Oh, Jesus! Oh, Jesus! Please, Jesus!' This was the way I'd heard the people do it before when they'd been saved. After a while, I fell on the floor and started rolling around in my brand-new suit. This looked good; I knew it had to be convincing" (210). After more of the same, Mrs. Rogers tells Sonny that he made a valiant try, and he thinks, "I never felt so low in my life. Here I was lying and rolling on the floor all that time, and this woman was saying I was *almost* saved. I was really disgusted, and I just never went back there anymore. I felt that it wasn't worth the time and effort. If I couldn't convince this woman I was saved, I'd never get next to June; she'd never let her out of the house by herself. I just chalked it up to experience" (211).

Brown's tone of voice in this and in similar episodes is much like the innocent mockery of Washington Irving. Indeed, Sonny often plays Rip Van Winkle in his desire to turn off the annoyances and irritations of his world and rebel through sleep. He has something of A. B. Longstreet's brutal humor in him as well and some of the exaggeration of Davy Crockett. Most consistently, again like Simple, he plays Huck Finn, the unlettered sage, anti-pretense, anti-authoritarian, who makes his points by assuming a deadpan innocent stance: "A lot of times I used to wish that Dad would die and that Mr. Sam would marry Mama and be our father. Mr. Sam used to like Mama, and he was real nice. He believed everything I told him. Dad was real mean, and he didn't believe anything I told him. But Dad told Mr. Sam that if he ever came across our threshold again, he was going to kick him in the ass. Mr. Sam must have believed Dad, because he didn't come back any more" (53).

As with Twain, Sonny's innocent stances are not always used for comedy. When Sonny's parents visit him at the Youth House, Sonny jumps a white boy and calls him a "lying faggot." His father slaps his mouth, but his mother starts weeping over the fact that Sonny would use the word "faggot." Sonny starts eating a pear:

> Mama just kept on crying, and Dad couldn't do anything about it. I could have told Dad what to say to make Mama stop crying. I could even have told him something to tell her to make her smile. It would have been a lie, but it would have made Mama feel real good. But I didn't say anything. It wasn't my place to say anything. And Dad kept on holding her and saying stupid things to her and Mama kept on crying and I kept on eating the pear. (65)

His innocence here is deliberate helplessness. It lets the scene, pathetically, interpret itself.

Sonny is never actually helpless in his story, which is why he controls the telling of it absolutely. Like Simple, he is born to be in control. As soon as his education gets under way, his success story begins. He is a fusion of Ben Franklin and Horatio Alger, demonstrating that all one needs to survive in the wilderness is a practical education and a good brain. Sonny acquires a highly specialized education, which he shares with his readers as would a teacher, delivering lectures on street fighting, sheet stealing, car stealing, "ringing" cash registers, on the distinction between whores and prostitutes, on the "Murphy," a prostitution con game, and on all elements of the street code. Sonny educates us, but he cannot educate Pimp, whose practical education has surpassed his brother's, and who is headed for a young death. This is the deeper education which Sonny receives, that so many of the lives about him have been fated from the outset.

The role of fate in *Manchild in the Promised Land* gives the book its element of horror. The people around Sonny believe in fate; they play the numbers. Late in the book Sonny meets a little boy who wants to grow up exactly like Sonny. The boy disturbs Sonny because he knows that most of the characters in his story are going to grow up like their predecessors, the boys and girls with whom he played as a child, turning junkie and prostitute. At one point he answers his mother that he doesn't know what is going to happen to him, and that there was "nothing [he] could do about it anyway" (67). All of *Manchild in the Promised Land* seems doomed from the start, which is why even Sonny's love is not enough to save Pimp from his own private horror story.

Here, as in *Native Son*, time and fate cooperate in sustaining the horror. Again, the idea emerges that the knowledge of time makes no difference to the characters, and the irony of Sonny's working in a watch repair shop, like Bigger's desire for a gold watch, is self-evident. There is, moreover, the ghostly figure of Father Time, reminiscent of Hardy, a walking-dead drug dealer who prowls Harlem as the embodiment of fate. For Sonny there are also the additional horrors of murderous policemen, continuous beatings, of violence as a way of life ("I was afraid of almost everything"), of the unpredictable explosions of his father, poverty, the persistent atmosphere of war, and the loneliness created by all these.

Overriding his specific fears are the larger ones of evil and madness. The novel begins in mischief and ends in crime. Sonny grows up with the problem of whether he can always understand the difference between them. As he gets older, the romance is squeezed out of his childhood pranks, as it is squeezed out of Harlem itself. Sonny feels certain that eventually he will have to kill somebody. He worries seriously about the meaning of the word "bad." Everyone around him is likewise worried about the nature of evil, about the existence of the devil within one's character, about "working roots" and the evil eye.

Sonny also knows that the idea of badness is ambiguous in his world. Down South he is told that his Grandpa was "a real bad and evil nigger when he was a young man" (49), meaning that his Grandpa had the nerve to stand up to white men. The "bad nigger" in Harlem is often the local hero; in *Manchild in the Promised Land*, he is the murdered gangster, Jim Goldie, who had made it big. To Sonny, however, this idea was upside down: "The bad nigger thing really had me going. I remember Johnny saying that the only thing in life a bad nigger was scared of was living too long. This just meant that if you were going to be respected in Harlem, you had to be a bad nigger; and if you were going to be a bad nigger, you had to be ready to die. I wasn't ready to do any of that stuff. But I had to. I had to act crazy" (127).

Madness is the other terror which besets him. Repeatedly in *Manchild in the Promised Land* the axiom of black fiction is demonstrated that to be crazy is to be sane in a mad situation. In detention, the boys set their house afire in order to be considered crazy, and thus get better treatment. The people who do the most to help others in the book are the ones called "crazy." Sonny is called crazy for talking back to the judge. It is said to be crazy to love a whore, and Sonny is thought to be crazy when he speaks of wanting to become a psychologist. To be crazy in *Manchild in the Promised Land* is ordinarily to provide what is honest or desirable.

Yet there is also the genuine craziness of self-destruction by drugs, of ending a life like Pimp, nodding in an ironic and pathetic affirmative. This is the craziness which Sonny most fears, being out of control of his own life. He fears Harlem because he knows Harlem to be his past and future. The Promised Land is in reality a wasteland—to "waste" means to kill in street language—and when at one point he finds himself seated in Hamburger Heaven, he sees exactly how much of paradise he has gained. The book begins with the sheet-stealing scene, and Sonny receives a warning, "Run!" He answers, "Where?" which is rhetorical until the end of the book when he leaves Harlem for good. "Look man," he says to a friend, and himself, "we aren't destined" (426).

Sonny survives his promised land. Taken strictly as a fictional hero, he survives almost exclusively on tone. Told any other way, the events of *Manchild in the Promised Land* would appear to be tragedy or fantasy—indeed, the final observation of the book is that it was all quite unbelievable—but humor, instead of lightening or diminishing the reality of the events, in fact intensifies it. In a sense, by making something humorous of that reality, Brown takes it as a given. The reader does not wonder whether or not to believe the narrative, but is relieved of the question by the author's perspective. This is Hughes's method with Simple, and it is Brown's as well.

We do not really care about Sonny or Simple, as we do about John Grimes and Sandy, because it is clear to us that both characters are in charge of their educations, and can take care of themselves. Both are equipped with a sense of humor which sets them above the situations which they report, and on which they make comment, and they rise above their own human vulnerability as well. Freud said that the pleasure of humor derives from "an economy of expenditure in feeling." Sonny and Simple escape from their cycles and flourish by keeping us away from our feelings. In the end we only really care about the inescapability of what was left behind. The exceptions prove the rule.

4
White
Outside

The sense of personal and social restriction under which the characters in black fiction operate is affected, if not entirely formed, by the fact that they almost always perceive themselves in terms of white expectations. No matter how contemptuous they may be of the quality of those expectations, or of the larger situation which made those expectations so powerful, very few characters in black fiction ever shake off the feeling that they are continually functioning in the sight of external judgment. Life in white America both lies outside their various cycles and is the cause of them. Accordingly, the thoughts and actions of the characters occur within what Du Bois called a "double-consciousness," which reflects and maintains the separation between America and black America in their minds.

Despite the width of this separation, however, despite the fact that it was imposed by the larger culture upon the smaller, and that it was created and is maintained by the subordination of the smaller to the larger, no black hero ever expresses the desire to join the majority. He may be desperate because of his blackness, and he may realize that his desperation is due to the condition of being supervised, directly or otherwise, by those who despise him; nevertheless, he does not wish to save himself by being as good as the whites, or as rich as the whites, or like the whites in any way, except possibly in the ability to live without constant fear. In most cases what his situation has taught him is that the source of his desperation may be worse off than he.

Over and over in this literature one listens to the various black characters talk compassionately, or with benign amusement, about how helpless white folks are. This is true not only of the older people and "handkerchief heads," but of the younger characters as well. White folks do not know how to grow their own crops, cannot raise their own children, are unable to deal with adversity, seem incapable of understanding the emotions of others, and even their own. As Aunt Hager says, it has been the lot of black people to correct or mitigate these deficiencies, not merely during the period of their slavery, but afterward, in fact forever. They must teach the white man not only how to survive, but also how to live comfortably within his wrong-doings; indeed, they must absolve him. In "Long Black Song" (*Uncle Tom's Children*) Sarah keeps thinking of her cynical seducer salesman as a helpless innocent.

Few black heroes think of the whites who abuse them so charitably, but the general conception of the white world in black fiction is the same as Sarah's: that it is a weak, dull (colorless), and morally impoverished world, populated mostly by terrorized people who demonstrate their terror-ized states of mind in their violence to others. A man who lives in accordance to the dictates of such people, and at the same time acknowledges his own moral superiority to them, begins to wonder about himself. On the one hand, he is free of the situation he recognizes by observing the corruption of his oppressors. On the other, he is largely defined by his oppression, his hopes and ambitions arising from the depths of his deprivation. When he attempts to understand himself, therefore, there must always be an equal effort to understand those who have kept him down. In fact, his conclusions about the outside world will often answer his deepest questions about himself.

The Uncalled

One of the most effective early novels to deal with the white outside world is Paul Laurence Dunbar's *The Un-called*. Dunbar has been regarded by almost everyone who comments on him as an accommodationist writer, and ex-cept for his celebrated poem "We Wear the Mask," nothing in his writing, and he wrote a great deal, seems to challenge the designation. Like *The Uncalled*, two of his other books, *The Love of Landry* and *The Fanatics*, are concerned with white characters and are addressed to a white audience. A fourth book, *The Sport of the Gods*, has blacks as its main characters, but the only discernible message for blacks which the book offers is that one ought not to migrate to the sinful North, but rather stay in the South and support the agricultural economy. *The Uncalled* (1898), Dunbar's first novel, is, however, quite different from the ones which followed. Unlike *The Love of Landry* and *The Fanatics*, it takes a steady and critical look at a white community, and despite its gentleness, in many ways it is the first successful protest novel in black fiction.

The white community of *The Uncalled* is a small Ohio town called Dexter. Freddie Brent's mother has died. His father, the town drunk, had run off years before. Freddie is left an orphan. The women of the town convene to decide where the boy will live. To everyone's surprise, the spinster Hester Prime volunteers to take custody of him, "but I want you to understand that it ain't a matter of pleasure or desire with me; it's dooty" (29). Miss Hester, whose motto is "Everything in order," strictly regulates Freddie's life, constantly reading the Bible and *Pilgrim's Progress* to him. She is courted by Eliphalet Hodges, who brings some humor and easiness to Freddie's upbringing, and in whom Freddie finds a second father. Eventually Freddie becomes infatuated with Elizabeth Simpson, the minister's daughter, who throughout the novel always seems to be humming a tune. Miss Hester urges Freddie to become a minister himself, and reluctantly Freddie allows himself to be prepared to succeed the Reverend Mr. Simpson.

Eliphalet Hodges had promised himself that whenever his faithful mare died, he would choose that moment to propose marriage to Miss Hester. Dunbar avoids suggesting the exact relationship between the two events, but the mare does die and the marriage occurs. Freddie meanwhile declares his love for Elizabeth, and except for the single transgression of playing baseball on Sunday, he sticks to the straight and narrow, which is the way Elizabeth wants it. Freddie delivers a brilliant guest sermon, and his future seems assured, until an issue arises between Simpson and himself involving the treatment of a local girl who had been made pregnant and had run from the town. The Reverend Mr. Simpson instructs Freddie to hold the girl up in church "as a fearful example of evil-doing" (181), but Freddie is more compassionate. Simpson then threatens to take the pulpit away from Freddie, and even suggests that the son of a drunkard may actually be the unnamed man in the story, whereupon Freddie turns on Simpson in a wild scene in church, and resigns his pastorate on the spot. Elizabeth immediately leaves Freddie, having tried to make him into something he was not, and Freddie, with the new understanding that Miss Hester had been doing the same, leaves Dexter for Cincinnati.

There, Freddie finds himself a rooming house, and takes up with another boarder, Perkins, who shows him the city. Freddie decides that he is going to become an author, and takes to the streets "on a search for characters." One night, accompanying Perkins to a beer garden, he is dissuaded from entering by a man outside the garden who instead convinces Freddie to attend a temperance meeting that evening. At the meeting Freddie listens to this man, known as the California Pilgrim, recount his life story, particularly his desertion of his wife and child. At the end of the speech, someone calls out to the California Pilgrim as "Brother Brent," and Freddie, who has been persistently haunted by his past, collapses at the discovery of his father. Weeks afterward, Eliphalet Hodges journeys to Cincinnati to tell Freddie that his father has returned to Dexter and wishes to see him. Freddie arrives at his father's deathbed in time to forgive all. In the final chapter, referred to as a nine day's wonder, Freddie is reunited with Christianity, falls in love with a girl named Alice, marries, and lives happily afterward.

As if the novel might not be moral enough as it is, Dunbar laces the narrative of *The Uncalled* with his own homilies and advice on a great variety of subjects. Country funerals are sardonically approved of for their brevity and lack of high cost. Motherhood is declared to be the only natural state of women. The education of children begins at too early an age: "It is not an unusual thing for mothers to send their babes off to kindergarten as soon as they begin to babble, in order to be relieved of the responsibility of their care" (36). There are maxims about human nature: "Freddie's training was the apotheosis of the non-essential. But, after all, there is no rebel like Nature. She is an iconoclast" (57). There is also a defense of the seriousness of puppy love. The civilizing effects of young women on young men are analyzed and praised. Shallow women are deplored: "It is one of the glaring sarcasms of life to see with what complacency a shallow woman skims the surface of tragedy and thinks that she has sounded the depths" (121). Finally, on growing old: "Life's turbulent waters toss us and threaten to rend our frail bark in pieces. But the swelling of the tempest only lifts us higher, and finally we reach and rest upon the Ararat of age, with the swirling floods below us" (248).

As for the moral lessons of the whole, two simple conflicts predominate. First, there is Freddie's freedom of personality pitted against Hester's choice of a way of life for him and the town's conception of propriety. His guest sermon, which uses "Judge not, that ye be not judged" as its text, signals Freddie's break from the town and from the church, and Freddie's speech against Simpson confirms it:

> To-night I feel for the first time that I am myself. I give
> you back gladly what you have given me. I am no
> longer your pastor. We are well quit. Even while I
> have preached to you, I have seen in your hearts your
> scorn and your distrust, and I have hated you in secret.
> But I throw off the cloak. I remove the disguise. Here
> I stand stripped of everything save the fact that I am
> a man; and I despise you openly.   (187–188)

The second conflict is between agrarian and urban life, a contest won by the country by means of a number of elaborate pastoral descriptions. In *The Uncalled* industry and the city are always invaders, even when those invaded are the landed gentry:

> Half-way up the hill, where the few aristocrats of the
> place formerly lived in almost royal luxuriance and
> seclusion, a busy sewing-machine factory has forced
> its way, and with its numerous chimneys and stacks
> literally smoked the occupants out; at their very gates
> it sits like the commander of a besieging army, and
> about it cluster the cottages of the workmen, in
> military regularity.   (106)

When Freddie leaves Dexter, he has no personal regrets, but he is wistful about the countryside. Walking through the crowded Cincinnati streets, he wonders, "Was this the humanity he wanted to know?" (207).

The ideas of the novel are obviously stated. Personal freedom is preferable to a narrow conception of duty, and the two are invariably opposed. Fate and free will are likewise in perpetual antagonism, and fate will out (it is Freddie's fate to be hounded by the reputation of his father, yet his reconciliation with his father is fated as well). Consistent with the arguments against unreasonable personal restraints is the opposition to artificiality generally. The still-to-be-reformed Miss Hester planted her garden "with such exactness and straightness that the poor flowers looked cramped and artificial and stiff as a party of angular ladies dressed in bombazine. Here was no riot nor abandon in growth" (32). It takes Freddie's rebellion to make Hester see Dunbar's Romantic thesis, that beauty in human and external nature lies in allowing nature to take its course and in a haphazard harmony of the whole. Freddie is called handsome for his "irregular features."

All of the characters in *The Uncalled* are white. The only reference to blacks in the novel occurs when Freddie observes the Cincinnati street scene: "A quartet of young Negroes was singing on the pavement in front of a house as he passed and catching the few pennies and nickels that were flung to them from the door" (207). The activity is innocent enough, and might even arouse the reader's compassion, yet Freddie is "sickened, disgusted, thrown back upon himself" (207) by the noise and confusion. His reaction dismisses the scene and thereby dismisses the one aspect of the novel, other than the identity of its author, which might openly connect it with black life. Yet the connection is there.

There is, first of all, the novel's association of whiteness with death and terror. It is snowing on the day of Margaret Brent's death. White flowers are brought to the body, and a white cloth covers a cracked mirror in her home. Then there is the pervasive sense of inevitability, which hangs over Bob Jones (*If He Hollers Let Him Go*) and Bigger, and dominates Freddie as well. Like most black heroes, Freddie is without the companionship of a father. He has no heritage to draw on, yet lives with the town's supposition that he has a built-in inherited weakness. He is heading toward a prescribed life in the church. At times he refers to himself as a slave. Like Elisha in the Temple of the Fire Baptized, he "walks disorderly," and is upbraided for straying. His conversion is no more sincere than Gabriel's or Manchild's. When he rises from the mourners bench to "get religion," it is an act of expediency to please the elders and Miss Hester.

There are also continual references to Freddie's breaking his bonds. Someone says of Freddie, "A panther cub ain't going to be a lamb." And there are all the inevitable allusions to Exodus. Dunbar describes his hero as

> a boy strong and full of blood. The very discipline
> that had given a gloomy cast to his mind had given
> strength and fortitude to his body. He was austere,
> because austerity was all that he had ever known or
> had a chance of knowing; but too often austerity is but
> the dam that holds back the flood of potential
> passion. Not to know the power which rages behind
> the barricade is to leave the structure weak for a
> hapless day when, carrying all before it, the flood shall
> break its bonds and in its fury ruin fair field and
> smiling mead. (79)

The value of language is played down against the value of feeling, as it is in *Go Tell It on the Mountain*, *Home to Harlem*, and elsewhere. The central theme of the book is the destructive effect of human prejudice; "Judge not, that ye be not judged" (153).

Nothing in the novel is so characteristic of black fiction, however, as the nature of Freddie's rebellion. When Freddie defies the congregation, he says that for the first time in his life he is himself, that while he has endured the town's whispered hatred of him because of his lineage, he too has secretly hated the town. But now, "I throw off the cloak. I remove the disguise" (188). This outburst is particularly telling coming from Dunbar, who throughout his career was patted on the head by white critics, including William Dean Howells, who always insisted that Dunbar remain a pleasant and inoffensive dialect poet. Dunbar created his own modulated outburst in "We Wear the Mask," in which he deplored the "debt we [blacks] pay to human guile" by smiling in spite of "bleeding hearts" and by mouthing "myriad subtleties." *The Uncalled* itself may be one of those subtleties.

Despite the light-handed moralizing, the convenient coincidences, the sudden and all-encompassing happy ending, and all the other stilted or facile elements of the book, *The Uncalled* is at bottom a severely critical novel. When Freddie asserts, "Here I am stripped of everything save the fact that I am a man," he is not merely taking a personal stand, but is proclaiming his membership in a common human brotherhood, the idea of which is scorned by those he is addressing. On the city streets Freddie condemns the "low life" about him as being subhuman. It takes the reappearance of his father, and his own consequent understanding of his father's plight and suffering, to make Freddie aware of his common humanity.

Yet Freddie must learn this truth on his own, and in an antipathetic context. The townspeople of Dexter offer him only resistance, learn nothing from the church episode, and continue living in a restricted society governed by a narrow theology. In Dexter Dunbar is portraying his perception of the white world. He is depicting a people who, while pretending to adhere to principles of decency and to maintain an egalitarian world, efficiently and systematically stifle the freedom and honesty of an individual different from themselves, and do so in a quiet and often charming manner. In Freddie's case the quality of difference is that he is the son of a drunkard and therefore cursed as being unfit for God or town. If he were black, he would be considered unfit for more than that, and for the same lack of reasons. Meanwhile, the town, the state, goes on unaffected toward greater moral constriction and deeper fear of the individuals within.

In his essay "Negro Character as Seen by White Authors," Sterling Brown criticized Roark Bradford's *Ol' Man Adam and His Chillin*, Marc Connelly's source for *Green Pastures*, by pointing out Bradford's facile and cruel classifications of black people. Brown used Bradford "to show how obviously dangerous it is to rely upon literary artists when they advance themselves as sociologists and ethnologists," and went on to examine the extent to which the black man had been pigeonholed in American literature up to 1933, when the essay was written. The stereotypes Brown classified were these: (1) the Contented Slave, (2) the Wretched Freeman, (3) the Comic Negro, (4) the Brute Negro, (5) the Tragic Mulatto, (6) the Local Color Negro, and (7) the Exotic Primitive. He analyzed the literary abuses under each classification in order to show how the depictions of blacks, most of which were ostensibly devised to contribute to racial understanding, actually served to exacerbate racial problems.

Brown blamed black authors as well as white for the practice of stereotyping, and also cited exceptions to his thesis on both sides; but his particular indictment of white authors was accurate at the time it was written, and would be so now. With the individual exceptions of Melville (*Benito Cereno*), Gertrude Stein (*Malanctha*), Faulkner, and perhaps Twain, and conceding some others whom Brown himself cited, Eugene O'Neill, Howard Odum Ridgeley Torrence, Julia Peterkin, and Thomas Wolfe, there have been very few sustained and serious delineations of black characters by white American writers. In most cases in American literature generally, where white characters have contact with black, the black character functions under one or another of Brown's classifications or, as in *Tender is the Night*, is presented too fleetingly to be interesting or understood.

The opposite situation is, however, not true. Chester Himes creates a penetrating and sympathetic study of the white Maggie in *If He Hollers Let Him Go*. John Williams covers a whole range of the thoughts and actions of white characters as they deal with black in *The Man Who Cried I Am*. Baldwin covers a wider range in *Another Country*. Even McKay, for all his enthusiasm for the primitive, does quiet justice to his whites, portraying them as complicated people. More than other black writers, Wright is apt to treat his white characters as a collective in the abstract, but his complex and tortured district attorney in *The Outsider* is no abstraction. The interesting contradiction here is that despite the care taken by almost every black author not to reduce his white characters to stereotypes, there nevertheless emerges within black fiction a consistent picture of white America. What was true for Dunbar at the turn of the century has evidently been true for most black authors writing afterward.

Like *The Uncalled*, Ann Petry's *Country Place* is concerned with the narrowness and maliciousness of small town life, the town in this instance being Lennox (Old Saybrook), Connecticut, and the time, 1947. The story is narrated by the local druggist, Doc, an *Our Town* common-sense character who sees and hears all, and is centered on Johnnie Roane and his wife, Glory. Johnnie has returned from World War II, and is now eager to study art in New York. Glory does not wish to leave Lennox, partly because she feels comfortable there, and partly because she wants to develop her love affair with Ed Barrell, the local stud. On Johnnie's first night home, Glory turns away from him. When at the end of the story Johnnie discovers Glory's infidelity, he turns from her, freeing himself from Lennox as Fred Brent had freed himself from Dexter.

The subplot of *Country Place* involves Mrs. Gramby, the matriarch of the town, who, like Johnnie, seeks to free herself from the town's worst attributes. Mrs. Gramby represents New England elegance and tradition. In her weak son's marriage to Lil, Glory's mother, she envisions the eventual disintegration of her standard of living. In a series of events which in summary read like soap opera, but which are presented convincingly in the book, it is revealed that Lil too has had an affair with Ed. Lil, wanting to inherit the Gramby house, poisons Mrs. Gramby, but fails to kill her. In the end, Mrs. Gramby revises her will, bequeathing Johnnie Roane enough money to get out of Lennox. Leaving her lawyer's office, Mrs. Gramby and Ed Barrell are on the staircase together. Mrs. Gramby trips and pushes Barrell in front of her as she falls, ending both lives at once.

Among the many minor characters in the book, the cab driver called The Weasel is the most complete. A poisonous figure, not unlike O'Casey's Joxer, though without Joxer's range of cleverness, it is he who arouses Johnnie's suspicions of his wife, and he too who discovers and reveals Lil's former relationship with Ed. Ed himself, "good old Ed," is a bull with a bad heart, an empty man who serves as the town's last symbol of procreation and, ironically, runs its gas pump. He uses women and sells used cars: "All roads lead to Rome. Rome is a filling station. Rome is Ed Barrell and his bowlegs and his bulging chest and his leaky heart" (120). The only black character in the novel is the Gramby's maid, Neola, who is also the only free person in the cast. Lil thinks, "If Neola was white and didn't have that dead pan expression on her face, she wouldn't be bad looking. Not anything to rave about, but she'd get by in a crowd" (61). In truth Lil envies Neola, who is loved by the "Portugee" gardener, whom she eventually marries in the book's single happy event. As Lil "watched their faces she thought, bitterly, the whole town is happy, everybody but me" (62).

Of course the point of *Country Place* is that the town is not happy. It is an aggregation of terrified individuals, anti-black, anti-Semitic, anti-Catholic, and anti-themselves, who simultaneously seek solace in each other and each other's annihilation. In such a setting Glory reigns like the local teen-age beauty queen, her name containing all the promise of small town America, indeed the flag itself, her character containing nothing but the desire for cheap excitement and easy comfort. Her husband wishes to become an artist, but there can be no art in Lennox. Lennox has worked itself into a corner where no one is free to act upon principle or conscience: "When Neola brought the tea, Mrs. Gramby poured a cup for Lillian, and one for

herself. She sipped the tea, thinking, This is proof of the
great advance of our civilization, this pouring tea for a
woman I despise, a woman I hate, when what I want to do
is turn her out of the house" (156). Mrs. Gramby's decision
to give her house to Neola and the "Portugee" is in a sense
her revenge on Lennox, but Lennox, like Dexter, is not
available to revenge or to any form of education. It is a
country place, the place that the country has reached, and
it is locked in that place by its own limited vision.

The chief characteristic of that vision, the essence of
its limitation, is that it is without real imagination. What
passes for inspiration in the town are rumors or daydreams
informed by Hollywood, by the sense of high melodrama
in which people rise to great and false passions, elation and
despair, at the most insignificant and superficial impulses.
This is the level of imagination to which Johnnie Roane is
drawn, and the one he intuitively wishes to avoid. Before
his confrontation with Ed Barrell, he pleases and appeases
Glory by changing his mind about leaving Lennox, convincing himself that this change is right because "that
night Glory slept in his arms . . . The wind, the damp cold,
Ed Barrell, could no longer touch him now. Nothing could
touch him now because he had Glory. Just before he went
back to sleep, he decided that he had never lost her anywhere except in his imagination" (131).

In fact, the capacity of Johnnie's imagination is at
issue, the question of whether that capacity will be filled
with demonstrations of the gaudy American dream represented by his wife, whose idea of heaven, and drama, is
movie-made—a cozy cabin, a roaring fire, and the embraces
of star-crossed lovers—or with genuine art, the art Johnnie
seeks. In his anger Johnnie hoists Glory and Ed to epic and
dramatic heights: "He [Ed], the Lennox Lothario, the
Romeo of the filling station. He and Glory of the bright
hair, of the hair like a golden net, were now Romeo and
Juliet, were playing at Tristan and Isolde" (185). The allusions are an obvious mockery, as he admits to himself when
he is about to board the train for New York: "You're dodg-
ing as usual, he thought, ducking even the saying of her

name. Glory. Say it. Repeat it. Glory. That's her name. She was the soapbubble, the dream, the illusion, the bright hope" (247). The acknowledgment implies that whatever Johnnie will become as an artist will depend on how he deals with reality, just as Petry herself is saying that it is the perpetuation of fantasy which has made Lennox so lifeless.

In a sense, Johnnie got his first taste of reality by means of fantasy, specifically Glory's. Peering through the cabin window at his wife and Ed, he is desperate to get to them. But he stumbles around in the mud for a long time, and cannot find the door, which is also the door to Glory's mind. There is a certain degree of shock and outrage in the initial discovery of his wife's infidelity, but it is surface outrage, born in part of the knowledge that Johnnie, too, had once been an actor in Glory's American dream, and now has been ousted from his part like an old ham. The more shocking and important discovery is that since his marriage he has grown outside of Glory's sensibility, and cannot get back in even when he thinks it necessary to do so.

But Lennox is more than unreal. The deeper and more abiding deficiency of the town is the absence of a usable past. On the first night after Johnnie came marching home, "He lay down in the black walnut bed and stared up at the carved grapes on the high headboard. He distinctly remembered when his mother bought the bed for him. He was fifteen and growing fast and she said he needed a man-sized bed. She had found this huge affair at an auction sale and had been furious because his father had said, 'Enough to give the boy nightmares. I bet whole families have died in that bed'" (28). The bed, in which Johnnie awaits the company of Glory, is Johnnie's history, a means of connection to tradition which is important to him now. It is not important to Glory, however, or to her mother, or to Ed. These others are the advocates of novelty, of new acquisitions, new love affairs, and new starts, which in turn are supposed to signal new characters and new lives. At tea Mrs. Gramby muses and reaches back for history:

Man had come a long and futile way. He had crawled
up out of the ooze and the muck only to fall back,
to get up and try again, and finally he had walked,
stood erect and walked, built cities, left them, gone
into a wilderness, founded churches, hunted witches.
Was it for this? And then there were the wars, for he
fought Indians, the French, the Dutch, the English;
and then later fought a Civil War, the Spanish, fought
in Europe, once, and then later fought again in
Europe and in Asia—yes, a long and futile way."
(157–158)

Specifically, she is reaching for American civilization, but
she cannot get a grip on the meaning of the past. She
bequeaths her house (tradition) to Neola and the "Portugee," in one more "futile" gesture. At the end it is still
Glory who inherits the earth.

The irony, for Petry, is that insofar as American civilization has tended toward any single purpose, it is precisely
so that the Glorys may be permitted to inherit the earth.
They, after all, are the "free" people, the logical followers
of Jefferson, Franklin, Emerson, and Whitman. Glory is, as
Ransom says of Philomela, persistently more young, and
not to be tied to any man, name, or heritage. In the context of black fiction her existence speaks for the need of a
heritage. Neola, on the other hand, whose name is an
anagram for "alone," has no history to build a life on. How
does a people needing and seeking a past find one in a
country which denies the value of the past? This is the
central problem of Country Place, and the kind of question which perpetuates the cycles of black fiction as a
whole.

dem

In Country Place and The Uncalled, heroes become
heroes by resisting, and eventually removing themselves
from, their environment. In William Kelley's novel dem,
the hero is his environment, and he perpetuates it. Here
the scene is New York City. The depiction of the white

world is larger and more intricate than Petry's or Dunbar's, but at bottom it is the same picture brought up to date. Kelley begins his novel with an epigraph in dialect: "næv, lemi telja hæv dem foks liv ... " (13). In *The Fire Next Time* (1963), Baldwin said that "white people cannot in the generality be taken as models of how to live. Rather, the white man is himself in sore need of new standards, which will release him from his confusion and place him once again in fruitful communion with the depths of his own being," which is what Dunbar and Petry implied. By 1967, however, Kelley is wondering if there is anything in the depths left to be excavated.

The plot of *dem* seems out of control, as do most of its characters. Mitchell and Tam Pierce live in a luxurious Manhattan apartment with their son, Jakie, and maid, Opal. Mitchell is an advertising man. The novel begins with him and a co-worker, Godwin, trying to devise a television commercial for a room deodorant called Heces. Godwin, an ex-Marine who had enjoyed the Corps because in it "you didn't have to pussyfoot around ... you killed or screwed anything yellow and talked to anything white" (27), tells Mitchell that he is being called up for active duty again. This has caused a domestic squabble because Godwin's wife is against the idea. Godwin invites Mitchell to his home on the weekend, and Mitchell, who admires Godwin, persuades Tam to go along. When they arrive, they discover that Godwin has murdered his wife and two children. Mitchell panics and freezes at the discovery, but Tam takes charge of the situation, tells Godwin to call the police, and leads her husband away.

Four months later Tam is pregnant. The Pierces take their summer vacation in Truro, on Cape Cod. In an attempt to impress a girl who is sunbathing on the beach, Mitchell jogs, trips, and breaks his ankle. He spends most of September in bed, and becomes absorbed in a television soap opera entitled "Search for Love." Mitchell is particularly taken with the heroine of the serial, Nancy Knickerbocker, "who was thirty-three, a year younger than Mitchell Pierce" (73), and with whom he vicariously falls in love. Meanwhile, back in the real world, it is clear to the reader, though not to Mitchell, that Tam has been having an affair for some time. When Mitchell returns to work, he begins to schedule his appointments in order to clear the time to watch his favorite program.

Mitchell's ardor for "Search for Love" is rewarded one evening when he chances to see the actress who plays Nancy Knickerbocker. He takes to spying on her, and eventually gets the opportunity to "rescue" her from her ex-husband, with whom she is having a drunken street brawl. In his ultimate glory, Mitchell sleeps with his dream woman. Afterward, he wants to run away with Nancy (whose real name is Winky Mendelblum), but Nancy, who realizes whom she is dealing with, gets rid of Mitchell by invoking a soap opera circumstance, and telling Mitchell that she must return to her husband who is "all alone, a broken man" (110). Mitchell goes home to Tam. Tam gives birth to twins, one black, one white, to everyone's astonishment but her own.

Earlier in the story, the Pierces had fired their black maid, Opal, for an alleged theft. Opal had also been reprimanded for allowing one of her boyfriends, Cooley, to call for her at the Pierce home. When Opal departed, Tam took up with Cooley, who, through the process of superfecundation, became the father of the black twin. The white twin is weak and dies. Naturally Mitchell cannot cope with any of this, but Tam's mother comes to his aid. She tells Mitchell to find Cooley, and pay him to take his child off their hands. Because Mitchell does not recognize Cooley when he meets him, he unwittingly enlists Cooley's services to uncover himself, whereupon Cooley fleeces Mitchell. In the end, Tam and Mitchell Pierce return home with their new black child. They decide to rehire Opal and pretend that she is the child's real mother, whom they have taken in.

The circular pattern of *dem* moves from brutality to fear to a sense of restriction, which creates an anesthetized condition, which develops into a feeling of entrapment or suffocation, which in turn becomes anger, which leads to brutality. The brutality is omnipresent in the novel, illustrated most dramatically in the character of Godwin. Godwin boasts that he knows dozens of ways to kill with his hands. Not only has he broken the necks of his wife and children, but he has raped the dead woman as well. The only craft which Godwin has mastered is murder, which is why he is eager to return to war. Not built for the advertising business, for secondary experience, he is the man of action and conquest who will desert (obliterate) his family ties in order to tackle the wilderness.

On the way to Godwin's house, the Pierces are entangled in a combination drag race and demolition derby with a road maniac, Ricco McInerney, whose dangerous game-playing foreshadows the revelation of Godwin's genuine insanity. The Vietnam war supports the television news, and goes on continuously in the background. There is an incidental anecdote which Mitchell hears from a cab driver, about how the driver murdered his captain in the war. Now the captain's shrunken head dangles over the cab's windshield. Mitchell listens to another anecdote in a bar, about a man who contracted gangrene and had to undergo a series of amputations: "at the end nothing was left but a head and a torso" (93). Mitchell pushes Opal to the kitchen floor when he accuses her of theft. And there is the sustained brutality shown by Mitchell to Tam, by Greg to Nancy Knickerbocker, by Cooley to Tam, Tam to Mitchell, and Cooley to Mitchell.

The brutality breeds fear, and everyone in *dem* is fearful of something. Tam is afraid of Jakie, her own son, and places the responsibility for his welfare upon Opal. The black policeman assigned to the housing complex where Opal lives is afraid that Mitchell has been sent to report on him. The fictional couple in the Heces ad are depicted as being afraid of being shunned by their neighbors because their house has odors. Opal is afraid of Cooley. Mitchell is afraid of almost everything: of a black man he passes on a walk in Central Park; of dirt (he folds his clothing neatly and washes his hands before making love to Nancy); of being conspicuous and different—he tells Godwin that during the war a Chinese girl unslanted her eyes for him; of being mistaken in his trivial decisions; of love; of appearing ruffled—he would rather expose his wife to danger in the Godwin home than appear to be shaken by the murder. Mitchell is particularly afraid of rejection: by his boss, by Godwin, whom he extols; by the other tenants of his apartment house who inquire about the twins; and by the doorman who may know the truth. The novel ends with Mitchell convincing himself, happily, that the doorman suspects nothing.

Fearful, the characters of *dem* deliberately contract their lives. Mitchell's Chinese girl falsifies her face and culture in the same accommodating gesture. The suburbia of Godwin's home is judged to be a domestic paradise, everyone to his own plot of land, and his own fences. Mitchell is a servant to his company, as Opal is a servant to the Pierces. The chief symbol of confinement is television, the low-culture universe in a box, in which realism consists only of moments of high intensity, and whose intention is to obliterate one's sense of reality, and discrimination, by bombardments of fake excitement. Here in the Evansdale (Dale Evans?) location of "Search for Love" is a whole cast of characters who do more than enough living, and suffer through more than enough complications, for everybody who observes them. Even a war is contained in that box; one does not have to leave one's house, like Godwin, to enjoy it.

The feeling of constriction takes the air out of the novel. Kelley's people are pictured as if functioning under ether: flopping about on beaches, enervated, squatting into easy chairs, widening as Opal widens out of shape, settling wherever they happen to be, like sheep. Sexual activity takes a great deal of effort, and love is never involved. When Tam understands that Godwin has raped his dead wife, she asks Mitchell if he would have done the same to her, if he would have loved her that much. Mitchell makes love to Tam reluctantly, particularly after he discovers Nancy, and Tam complains that she does not want to be "serviced" like a car. Cooley does "service" Tam, although he provides a bonus in the transaction. After the "rescue" scene, Nancy Knickerbocker asks Mitchell, "You're coming home to screw me, aren't you?" (98). The advertising business represents the anesthetizing of the imagination, as does "Search for Love." In the context of "Search for Love," the unreal and ridiculous, Mitchell is not fearful. There, at the level to which he was born, he becomes a rescuer of women in distress, a true lover and gallant gentleman: "I told my wife that I love you [Nancy] and that I'm leaving her and that we're getting married as soon as you and Greg are divorced" (109).

Mitchell does not want, nor is he able, to grow up, which is why he seeks mothers at every opportunity. Tam must take hold of him at Godwin's ("Say good-bye, Mitchell"), and only allows her husband to make love to her when she is certain that she controls the situation: "In bed she promised she would always take care of him" (51). Tam's mother must also take charge of Mitchell after the birth of the twins. A grotesque woman and a portent of Tam's future, she tells Mitchell how to act: "That's a good boy" (152). Opal mothers Mitchell as well: "I got hired to take care of you" (59). Even when Mitchell learns about "my Cooley" from Tam, he is incapable of any reaction but acquiescence:

> "I didn't know you'd take it this hard. Why, a couple of weeks ago you told me you didn't love me anymore. I thought you didn't care." She spread her arms to him. "I guess this is what they call a reconciliation." The sleeves of the white gown hung, like vestments. "Come here."
> For an instant, he held his ground, but then circled the bed, pulled up a chair and rested his head on her breasts, loose under the white gown. After all, he realized suddenly, he did love her.
> She put her arms around him. "Mitchell, you know I wouldn't have done all these terrible, terrible things unless you seemed to be falling out of love with me. You made me so desperate."
> His hand searched until it found her kneecap and

began to pat it. "I know, Tam. It's all right." Far down
the bed, her toes were wiggling under the blanket.
Between her thighs the black needles stuck up out
of the ball of pink wool.
    She kissed the top of his head. "Of course, it is.
Just the way it should be." (138)

In the final scene of the novel, Mitchell, thinking himself
safe from the doorman's suspicions, settles down into a
warm bath, making the ultimate return: "He turned out
the light and pulled down the shade. He sank down deep
into the hot water, and, on his side, his eyes closed and his
hands clamped between his thighs, he filled the darkness
with fantasies" (210).

Everyone is trapped in *dem*, and everyone wants out.
Mitchell wants to flee to paradise in Evansdale. Tam seeks
a form of escape in Cooley. The fictional Nancy Knickerbocker wants to achieve happiness by going to New York.
Godwin yearns to go back to the Marines. Wanting out
badly enough, they all panic and become desperate. Around
them, all the while, is the atmosphere of death. Tam's
stomach in pregnancy is compared to an Indian burial
mound. The doctor who informs Mitchell that his wife
has had twins is said to sound like a funeral director. The
bartender who tells Mitchell the story of the gangrenous
man marvels at how long the man lasted, "Jesus, Mary,
and Joseph, could that man die!" (91). The white twin dies,
though everyone's remorse is reserved for the black twin
who survives.

The general result of this entrapment is that people
become angry and seek vengeance. Tam wants to revenge
herself on Mitchell; at one point she "threatens" him with
her stomach. The black baby itself is an instrument of
revenge. Angered, everybody becomes brutal, and the circle
is complete. The black characters function in the same
circle. Cooley is brutal to Mitchell, not in using his wife,
who offered herself willingly, but by deceiving Mitchell.
Opal (a "jewel") is fearful of everyone, black and white.
Harlem itself provides the sense of constriction massively.
Demonstrating her etherized imagination, Opal has de-

signed her living room as a replica of the Pierce's. The black characters are entrapped, most are angry, and Cooley, particularly, seeks vengeance. He explains his impregnation of Tam as an assault on history, revenge for the time when Mitchell's forebears could do what they chose with the women of Cooley's.

The condition of slavery is the key to the novel, and the correspondences between the actions of the black and white characters occur within a context of slavery which applies to both. The circular shape of the book's activity occurs in slavery as well: people are brutalized; they become afraid; their fears are played upon by their constrictions; they become anesthetized for a time and do not care, until the accumulated years of the condition eventually bring on a sense of desperation, which causes anger and the desire for revenge, which leads to brutality. When Mitchell comes to Opal's house, to seek her aid in finding Cooley, the young black girls jumping rope in the street are singing,

> Sitting in a teepee, smoking a pipe.
> Polar bear come with a great big knife.
> Polar bear take and put us in a boat.
> So many children, thing couldn't float.
> Sitting in a boat, with a necklace of iron.
> Bear come down and say, "You're mine."
> Children start crying, raise up a noise.
> Everybody's crying, even the boys.
>
> Sitting in a cabin, smoking a pipe.
> The polar bear say I his wife.
> Take me by the hand and lead me out.
> Bear in the grass with a big cold snout.
> Sitting in a cabin, apron up high.
> So homesick I wish I could die.   (156–157)

The song is a slave song which connects blacks and American Indians at the short end of colonialism. Its point, which is the point of the novel, is that slavery corrupts everyone, the enslaver included.

Dem is about both ends of slavery, the black and white products of a nation founded in part on a slave economy. For the black, says Kelley, the question is, How does one deal with a false emancipation? For the white the trick is not to recognize that a system of slavery ever existed but rather to build up a network of self-exonerations in the name of civilization. Tam's mother announces to Mitchell, "We are the original people. Do you understand? Without people like us, this would be a lower-class Southern European slum. There would be no civilization at all. Those people ran from civilization, from education. We didn't. The real burden of maintaining civilization falls on us, especially on our women. The men may oversee the land, but we women maintain the culture" (146). The culture to which she refers is the one in which the enslaved Mitchell cannot recognize the enslaved Cooley, in which neither one has the desire or capacity to live with the other. If Cooley appears to have gotten the better of the Pierces, it is a pointless and ultimately Pyrrhic victory. The "culture" will always manage to place the black child where it feels it belongs.

In a mock summit conference on the problem of who keeps the baby meet Mitchell and Cooley, Pierce and Coolidge, bearing the weight of American history into the negotiations. The conference ends, as expected, in a status quo in which nobody finds what he is looking for because nobody knows what he is looking for. Kelley entitles the final section of his book "Twins," suggesting that Mitchell and Cooley are more alike than they care to know. Of the two other twins, the white one dies, just as Mitchell is "dead," and the black one survives, just as Cooley "survives," to become another orphan. Neither Mitchell nor Cooley is any good to himself or to the other, and both function within a paradox in which the dead exist to dominate the living, and the living exist to serve, destroy, or emulate the dead. As Mitchell drives to Opal's, he passes the scene of a car wreck on the highway. A huge black woman who has been thrown clear is seated on the grass, stunned, and shaking her head as if to ask, "How did I get here?" She is the emblem of her author's bewilderment.

One comes a long way from the Temple of the Fire Baptized to *Another Country*. Geographically, about five miles, from Harlem to Greenwich Village; spiritually, the distance from a depiction of the Saints to sinners of all varieties, and from a concentration on the straight and narrow to a survey of the wide open spaces of moral behavior. The context is modernity and the fact is sex. John, who may be on the rise at the end of *Go Tell It on the Mountain*, has been replaced as hero by Rufus, who kills himself at the outset of *Another Country*. Baldwin has largely dropped his biblical style, although some allusions remain. The sense of organization has changed as well: from focusing on individual characters, one by one, to a wide angle view of an entire people.

The title of the novel derives from one of three sources, and possibly from all of them. In Marlowe's *Jew of Malta* one of the friars confronts Barabas with "Thou hast committed . . . ," and Barabas interrupts him, and completes the accusation, saying, "fornication? But that was in another country, and besides the wench is dead." With a slight variation T. S. Eliot uses this exchange as an epigraph to his "Portrait of a Lady," a conversation between two people whose sophistication belies the fact that they are incapable of feeling. *Another Country* reflects the sterility and lovelessness depicted in Eliot's poem, and, like *The Jew of Malta*, is a revenge tragedy. The title could also come from a folk saying, "If a pigmy stands on a giant's shoulders, he can see another country," but the question of who is the pigmy, and who the giant, in this novel remains unanswered.

The central figure of the book is Rufus Scott, a black jazz drummer whose last days are spent tormenting Leona, a white Southern girl who loves him. Rufus is a desperate and degenerate man, made both by his various humiliations in the company of whites. He loves Leona, but has been reduced to a condition now where he can only hurt her. When he makes love to her, he deliberately turns the act into rape, as if to play out a classic fantasy. Eventually,

Leona goes mad, and partly out of remorse, partly because he has reached the bottom of his degradation, Rufus leaps to his death from the George Washington Bridge. Before dying he storms like Gabriel at the baptism: "He raised his eyes to heaven. He thought, you bastard, you motherfucking bastard. Ain't I your baby, too?" (78).

At Rufus' death, other characters take over: Vivaldo, the "Irish wop" from Brooklyn, Rufus' closest white friend, who wants to become a writer; Cass Silenski, a New England girl married to another writer, Richard, Vivaldo's former teacher; Eric Jones, an actor recently returned from France; and Ida Scott, Rufus' kid sister, a rising blues singer who seeks revenge against the white world for her brother's suicide. Ida moves in with Vivaldo, yet seeks to destroy him for letting her brother die. The implication throughout the novel is that all of Rufus' white friends, by sins of omission, allowed him to die.

Only Eric, the homosexual, is said to have brought love to Rufus which Rufus reciprocated; and when Eric and Rufus parted, Rufus was left destitute. Later in the story Eric is also said to bring love to Cass, who is drawn to him out of disgust with her marriage and Richard's vulgarity and shallowness. Eric is meant to symbolize a source of pure love for both sexes. He brings love to Vivaldo as well. In France, Eric finds his own love with Yves, a Paris street boy. The novel ends with Yves arriving in America at the New York airport, greeted by Eric, supposedly bringing with him a sense of sexual liberation which will herald personal and racial freedom for everyone involved.

Another Country is designed as a modern Inferno. Lovers throw themselves at each other in lust and violence. Rufus torments Leona, and Leona, merely by being white, torments him. Ida cheats on Vivaldo, and breaks his heart. Richard and Cass despise each other because of the falsity of their life, particularly of their artistic life. Ellis, the television executive who is going to launch Ida's career, treats Ida like a whore. Everyone betrays everyone else. Cass has an affair with Eric; Eric with Vivaldo; Vivaldo with Ida;

Ida with Ellis. In the character of Ellis is material gluttony. Sexual gluttony is ubiquitous. There is rape, in the rape of Leona. There is perversion and hysteria: Richard slams Cass in the head, and screams at her, "Did [Eric] make love to you better than I? Is that it? And did he fuck you in the ass, did he make you suck his cock? Answer me, you bitch, you slut, you cunt!" (316). There is even an implicit murder. At Rufus' funeral people glare at Vivaldo as if he had done the killing.

Baldwin sees the white characters as the prime, though not the sole, movers in all this evil. It is the white characters who have become unable or unwilling to probe the "dark side" of their human nature, the side which contains one's basic animalism and humanity as well, and which, if explored, might release these people from their self-made confinement. This confinement has made the whites brutal and rootless, whereas the black characters have been brutalized only by the whites, not by themselves, and so are morally cleaner. The black characters also suffer, but they understand the source of their suffering because they *are* the "dark side" of experience. The idea, put simply, is that blacks and whites must go to or create another country, in order to revamp or revitalize the one they have. Here is the deliberately arranged international cast: a Pole (Richard), a WASP (Cass), two blacks, an Irish-Italian, and a Frenchman. With them a new melting pot must be made, one characterized by personal and national freedom.

The structure of the novel consists of Book I, which focuses on the low and hopeless life (Rufus), and Books II and III, which represent a redemptive movement (Eric). Redemption is to be achieved by freedom on all fronts, especially sexual freedom. Homosexuality, in the person of Eric, becomes the main liberating force of the story. Blackness, too, is an expression of freedom, so blackness and homosexuality become thematically related. Book II begins with a picture of Eric in Eden: "Eric sat naked in his rented garden. Flies buzzed and boomed in the brilliant heat, and a yellow bee circled his head" (157). Eric is the new Adam, waiting for the arrival of Yves (Eve). Homosexuality, considered a vice, becomes a virtue, thus making a heaven of hell.

How stable a heaven homosexuality creates is problematical, however. The pervasive condition of *Another Country* is chaos, a chaos in which various freedoms oppose various restraints in search of a new order. Eric, who "had discovered, inevitably, the truth about many men, who then wished to drive Eric and the truth together out of the world" (180–181), is said to represent the new order, while everyone else floats in a vacuum of what Robert Lowell called "lost connections." In *Go Tell It on the Mountain* Baldwin's characters were islands inhabiting the island of Harlem. Here, there is the other island of Manhattan, and again the people are islands to each other. It is said that Rufus "made some very bad connections" (218), and it is fitting that he uses a bridge to end his life.

Ida's singing is also described as if it were an island, powerful and mysterious. Cass and Richard intentionally drift apart from each other. Richard will not speak Polish, wishing to deny and be free of his national identification. Everyone seeks to be a stranger, although at Rufus' funeral the mourners sing, "I'm a stranger, don't drive me away" (105), and Rufus' mother tells Vivaldo to visit them often, "Don't you be a stranger" (122). The goodbyes people share in the novel are always prolonged tediously, like the stringing out of a life-line. Homosexuality, too, creates a state of isolation in the unproductive act. People continuously speak of being exiled, and when Cass waves goodbye to Vivaldo it's "like waving goodbye to the land" (239).

The people are islands, and the islands are at war. Richard and Vivaldo are in a talent war, each striving to out-write the other. Rufus and Leona have inherited a state of war, which they continue. Cass and Richard are in a permanent battle; Ida fights Ellis, Vivaldo fights Ida, and so on. Even the young people are at war. The Silenski children are beaten in a gang fight with black children. Baldwin uses metaphors of war to describe the various relationships: battlefields, truces, retreats, treasons, triumphs, betrayals, wounds, loyalty, banishment, minefields. The epigraph of Book II—"Why don't you take me in your arms and carry me out of this lonely place"—is from Conrad's *Victory*. Vivaldo feels threatened among Ida's musician friends: "He had no function, they did: they pulled rank on him, they closed ranks against him" (270). When Ida makes love to Vivaldo, hers is the "technique of pacification" (148).

Because they exist in a state of war, all of the characters are wary and afraid. Leona is terrorized by Rufus, Rufus is terrorized by everyone, and everybody hides from everybody else out of fear of exposure. At the beginning of the story Rufus plays the drums accompanying a saxophone, and hears the repeated refrain, "Do you love me? Do you love me? Do you love me?" (13). On route to Rufus' funeral, the radio in Cass's taxi plays, "Love me." Vivaldo prays, "Oh God, make [Ida] love me." Yet, with all the talk of love, Rufus, wracked with hate and self-hate, is beyond connections. Leona, punchy from a brutal early marriage, cannot survive with Rufus, and ends up alone in madness. Richard is isolated in his literary pretensions, and despite his liberal protestations, is filled with race hatred. Cass, who married beneath her, cannot be honest with her husband. Vivaldo, who progressed from a Brooklyn street gang to the Village, has no place of his own, no ties. Ellis, the agent and impresario, has the loneliness of the parasite. Ida, bent on success and revenge, has objectives which demand secrecy and allow no trust in anyone.

The isolation of the characters from one another is complemented by their isolation as artists. Six of the major characters in *Another Country* are artists themselves, and all of the others live off of or with artists. Most of these artists are inept (the characters whom Vivaldo creates in his fiction do not "trust" him), but good or bad, being an artist is itself an insular condition. Except for Rufus, who occasionally is able to lose himself in his drumming, and Ida, who also occasionally can transport herself by singing, the rest of the characters function as spies, predators; actors, painters, and writers taking notes on experience, and gathering material second hand. In *Notes of a Native Son*

Baldwin said, "The only real concern of the artist [is] to recreate out of the disorder of life that order which is art." Instead of making order out of chaos, these artists accomplish the reverse.

Out of the chaos they create emerge Eric and Yves, who are said to bring emancipation to the new world. The notion is a curious turnabout as it relates to American thought. In his famous Phi Beta Kappa address, Emerson advised the nation no longer to court the muses of Europe, rather to shake off the degeneration of the old world in the name of fresh starts and native resources. In *Another Country* the apparent solution is to seek the European muse, thereby to free the new world of its moral imprisonments. The matter, to Baldwin, is the freedom to love: "When people no longer knew that a mystery could only be approached through form, people became—what the people of this time and place had become, what he [Vivaldo] had become. They perished within their despised clay tenements in isolation, passively, or actively together, in mobs, thirsting and seeking for, and eventually reeking of blood. Of rending and tearing there can never be any end, and God save the people for whom passion becomes impersonal" (255).

Eric, then, is supposed to bring love; yet for all the statements in his behalf, he is as alone as any of the others in the novel, and knowingly or not he has sent for Yves to share his loneliness. Eric may have "found himself"— that discovery is called his saving grace—but he has brought nothing lasting or revitalizing to those with whom he comes in contact. As Yves enters the country, he is anxious but reassured by the sight of Eric waiting for him on the airport's observation deck: "Then he was in a vaster hall, waiting for his luggage, with Eric above him, smiling down on him through glass. Then even his luggage belonged to him again, and he strode through the barriers, more high-hearted than he had ever been as a child, into that city which the people from heaven had made their home" (366). Eric welcomes Yves into the cage, into another country which will corrupt him.

At one point Cass confronts Ida with the possibility that things can change for the better. Ida responds that the cyclical pattern of history is strong enough to preclude change, and Cass thinks, "I don't believe it. . . . If you're talking of yourself and Vivaldo—there are other countries —have you ever thought of that?" (294). Ida scorns the idea, saying that by the time she and Vivaldo could raise the money to go, there would be nothing left of their feeling for each other. But her argument is academic. The truth is that there is no other country for Ida, Vivaldo, or any of these characters. It is America itself, says Baldwin, which is another country, one other than the country it believes itself to be. If these people, black and white, seek another country still, they must look inward.

The irony of such a message applies directly to the entire history of black writing. The first black novels produced in America concerned themselves with proving that black people were as good as the whites, as honorable, intelligent, and decent. The characters in the early novels were either as white in actual color as their authors could make them, or, as the line in "Black and Blue" goes, "white inside"; but the point was always the same, that day by day black people were becoming increasingly white because to become white was a sign of general improvement. By the 1920's, however, a writer like Walter White was leading his octoroon (*Flight*) back to her ghetto and away from the white world in which she had become uncomfortably assimilated. By 1940 Bigger Thomas and Lustre Johnson (of Ann Petry's *The Street*) were taking on the white world with murder in their hearts. And by 1960, Kelley and Baldwin, having come full circle with a twist, are again saying that their heroes and heroines are surviving because they have become just as good as the whites with whom they deal, just as self-seeking, treacherous, and dishonorable.

Seventy years intervene between Dunbar and Kelley, yet if there is any perceivable difference in the treatments of white America in their work, or in that of Petry and Baldwin, it is merely a difference of degree. In all four books art arises as an important force. Freddie Brent and Johnnie Roane wish to become artists because they believe they can remake the world. Mitchell Pierce, a writer for an ad agency, does not hold that belief. His "art" is commercial, as is the art of the characters in *Another Country*. As Baldwin says, art is supposed to shape life, but in these books the life has diminished the art within it, and has forced an accommodation which has made art unable to shape anything. The association of blackness with art is an association with a form of freedom, so the suppression of art becomes one more form of confinement. Without art, the world which is white outside is not only lifeless and self-destructive; it is, in terms of art itself, out of control.

5
The
Hero
Vanishes

The final effect of the cyclical patterns of black fiction is shown in the nature and progress of the hero. The question of heroism in this literature is a peculiar one because the contexts of the stories do not allow for much heroism, at least in its standard forms. Traditional or Romantic heroism is impossible within most of black fiction simply on the grounds that a Romantic hero, if he deserves his designation, has got to straighten out confusions, right wrongs, clear up perspectives, or, in the Byronic sense, rise godlike above his predicaments—activities which are rarely found in these stories. Janie of *Their Eyes Were Watching God* is a true heroine in the Charlotte Brontë mold because she endures well, holds on to her decency and sense in spite of the fakery about her, and triumphs over apparent defeat. In *Uncle Tom's Children* Wright's Mann ("Down by the River Side") and An' Sue ("Bright and Mornin' Star") take heroic stands, but neither character is complicated enough to allow his heroics to consist of anything more than brave deeds. Gabriel Prosser of Bontemps' *Black Thunder* fights heroically against enormous odds, though like Mann and An' Sue his heroism derives almost totally from valor. Yet even these are the exceptions. Generally the heroes of black fiction are not valorous, but terrified and introspective men and women who tilt at windmills on the percentage basis that more than half the time the monsters are real.

Largely because of that reality, black heroes are not standard anti-heroes either. No matter how they may fantasize about their threatened conditions or exaggerate the extent to which the world, specifically the white world, is plotting against them, the fact remains that their enemies, a lot of them, a lot of the time, are dangerous, and not imagined. This is the essential distinction to be made between the anti-heroes of Capote, Salinger, and so forth, and those in this literature. It is not that the enemies of modern white heroes are less oppressive in terms of what the heroes feel, but that these enemies, even when externalized, are theoretical and abstract. Whereas the enemies of the black heroes exist within history. When black heroes go up against them, they go up against history; and when they lose, as they almost always do, they lose to authentic facts of life.

Where modern black and white heroes come closest to each other in terms of common atmosphere and situations is in the literature of the existentialists. The various emphases found in modern existentialism are found in black fiction as well: the recognition on the part of the main character that he is an outcast from normal society; that the world is a perilous, wasted, or meaningless place; that as a product of a hostile environment he is afraid and divided in his personality; that consequently he needs to dissemble his false and real selves in order to discover who he is; and that he wishes both to live and to die with equal fervor.

The most prominent existentialist hero in black literature is Wright's Cross Damon, *The Outsider,* who through a series of philosophical negations and negative acts, including the desertion of his children and wanton murder, seeks to create his own frame of reference, in fact to make a god of himself. In essence he is like Melville's Pip, who left to drown by the white crew of the *Pequod,* "saw God's foot upon the treadle of the loom, and spoke it." Damon follows Nietzsche; if all the gods are dead, then man must accept, indeed seize, absolute responsibility, and the individual must be superior to any universal force. In this same sense Bigger is an existentialist hero, as is Saul, the hero of Wright's short story "The Man Who Killed a Shadow." Bereft of positive values, such characters create and celebrate negative values. Because they are black, and considered to be personifications of the negative, negative values would seem to be exactly what they need for self-fulfillment.

Yet even here there is a basic difference between the black existentialist hero and his white counterpart. It is questionable whether any black hero, Cross Damon or the Invisible Man, who is so much of an outcast that he disappears entirely, may properly be called existentialist when compared to the heroes of Beckett, Kafka, Malraux, Sartre, or Pirandello. Again, the difference lies in what is authentically true to both the hero and his reader, as opposed to what is true solely in the hero's mind. In Robert Musil's *The Man Without Qualities*, Moosbrugger commits his murders out of a desire to be let alone. Cross Damon, on the other hand, commits his murders out of the necessity to be alone, since the society of (white) men had made it impossible to survive otherwise. Similarly, Kafka's K is beset by allegorical creatures who function in abstract and dreamlike circumstances; whereas the Invisible Man's enemies, allegorical as their names may be, are real and have historical antecedents. In both sets of instances the nightmares are overwhelming, but only in one set do the heroes have the possibility of awakening.

The uniqueness of the black hero in modern fiction lies not only in his circumstances, but in how he deals with them as well. Insofar as existentialist literature is the literature of disorientation, then most black heroes may be called existentialist. Insofar as existentialist literature is the literature of despair, however, the black heroes do not qualify. On the whole, black heroes are hopeful characters. Whether they believe in a system, or try to beat it, or annihilate it and start from scratch, they are doers who, at least at the outset of their stories, act on high hopes of success. Even the introspective black heroes are not protagonists in the Aristotelian sense because whatever tragic flaws they may contain are more than counterbalanced by the communal flaws with which they struggle. Often the prime tragic flaw they detect in themselves is that their thoughts and actions confirm the expectations of their enemies, and lead to their downfall in spite of themselves.

This obedience to external expectations is, as the Wright-Harrison anecdote of Chapter One suggests, the most significant factor in these heroes' behavior. Heroes may start out thinking themselves to be in control of their lives, that is, to function in the subjective; but eventually they begin to see themselves as objects, specifically as objects created by others. Consequently, they become not unlike works of art in the ways they view their roles in the world. As art has been said to hold a mirror to life, so these characters, by satisfying white men's prescriptions, increasingly become mere reflections of the life about them.

Plato disparaged the value of art in the *Republic* by comparing it to a revolving mirror which, though it might reflect all things in nature, was not equal to any of them. This may be what Toomer is suggesting with the dwarf in "Box-Seat" who passes his mirror over the theater audience. The point is that the black heroes, despite strong efforts of resistance, gradually become mirrors themselves, and do not exist without the life outside them. When John Grimes studies his face in the mirror, or when the girls in "Kabnis" do the same, they are in a sense looking out of another mirror which is their lot. They do not exist without someone else telling them how, and so first lose their reason for being, and then their being itself.

If He Hollers Let Him Go

I aspire to the craziness of all honest men.

—LeRoi Jones, "Philistinism and the Negro Writer"

Bob Jones, the hero of Chester Himes's *If He Hollers Let Him Go*, relates the story of his life. Like all first-person narrators, he offers the reader the choice of believing him or not. The test of his reliability is made by the amount of detectable objective reality in the story, but reality in fiction, even in realism, is a matter of perception. A good many things happen in this novel, and it is up to us to determine whether there is any distance between what Bob tells us has happened and what happens in fact. Knowing that Bob is a little crazy does not make the problem easier.

He is living in a Los Angeles rooming house. His neighbor is Ella Mae Brown, a married woman with whom Bob is having an occasional and playful affair. He works as a leaderman, a middle-level supervisory position, in the Atlas shipyard. He is engaged to Alice Harrison, a social worker and daughter of a prominent black physician. At the outset of the novel everything is going very well for Bob, except that he dreams a great deal, and awakens terrified every morning.

Then Madge, a white woman from Texas who also works in Bob's shipyard, helps to change things around:

> She was a peroxide blonde with a large-featured, overly made-up face, and she had a large, bright-painted, fleshy mouth, kidney shaped, thinner in the middle than at the ends. Her big blue babyish eyes were mascaraed like a burlesque queen's and there were tiny wrinkles in their corners and about the flare of her nostrils, calipering down about the edges of her mouth. She looked thirty and well sexed, ripe but not quite rotten. She looked as if she might have worked half those years in a cat house, and if she hadn't she must have given a lot of it away. (21)

When Madge refuses to follow one of Bob's orders, declaring "I ain't gonna work with no nigger" (29), Bob calls her a cracker bitch. He is demoted for this. At lunch on the same day he joins in a craps game, and wins, but when he goes to take his money he gets into a fist fight with a white worker named Johnny Stoddart. Stoddart knocks Bob unconscious, and Bob vows to kill him. In two sudden events he has made a pair of sworn enemies.

From this point on, the novel becomes episodes. Bob follows Stoddart to his home and threatens him with a gun. He intentionally brings Alice to a restaurant not frequented by blacks, and the evening is a terrible failure, ending in Alice's taking Bob to visit a lesbian friend of hers. Alice apologizes later, and they are reconciled, but fall apart again when Bob cannot suffer the social pretenses of Alice's fellow social workers. Alice and Bob continue to squabble until Bob agrees to make some compromises with white people, even to the extent of making amends with Madge.

Madge, however, wants Bob more than his apologies; and when Bob comes to her apartment the two of them lock in a quasi-sexual wrestling match which ends with Bob running out of the house. The next day he promises to

The Hero Vanishes   165

straighten himself out again. He takes Alice's advice to become accommodating, cool his temper, and ask for his old job back. He vows that he will marry Alice, return to college; and become a great lawyer. He humbles himself before the boss who demoted him, and seeks to set things right with Madge one more time.

He discovers Madge napping in a dark room of a ship under construction at the yard. Because Madge is ever amorous, she begs him to stay. They argue and shout, and are overheard outside. Madge, now afraid of being caught with Bob, cries out, "Help! Help! My God, help me! Some white man, help me! I'm being raped" (170). Other workers rush into the room, and beat Bob unconscious. When he awakens, he escapes from his captors and phones Alice, who offers some more advice on the proper conduct of his life. Finally, he is recaptured and taken to trial, where he learns that the rape charge has been dropped: "I knew right off what had happened; they'd grilled Madge and learned the truth, or learned enough to guess at the rest. His [the president of the Atlas Corporation] conscience bothered him too much for him to let me take a strictly bum rap, but he'd never come right out and say it; he'd cover for her till hell froze over and make believe that he was doing it for the best. But I didn't care how he played it—I was beat" (190). The judge gives Bob the choice of jail or the army, and at the close of the novel Bob is off to war.

Those are the external events of *If He Hollers*, but the essential action of the story occurs within Bob's mind, the things he thinks as the action occurs. In certain ways Bob is not unlike Bigger Thomas. Himes wrote *If He Hollers* in the wake of the success of *Native Son*, and many similarities between the two books are deliberate. Both heroes are deeply self-conscious. Both contend with an accusation of rape which is false. Both undergo court trials with fated consequences. At one point Himes draws the parallel of the two books directly:

"*Native Son* turned my stomach," Arline said.
"It just proved what the white Southerner has always

said about us: that our men are rapists and murderers."

"Well, I will agree that the selection of Bigger Thomas to prove the point of Negro oppression was an unfortunate choice," Leighton said.

"What do you think, Mr. Jones?" Cleo asked.

I said, "Well, you couldn't pick a better person than Bigger Thomas to prove the point. But after you prove it, then what? Most white people I know are quite proud of having made Negroes into Bigger Thomases." (84–85)

As for the potential for violence in each hero, it becomes a question of how they deal with their fears. When Bigger is afraid, he acts to cover his fears. When Bob is afraid, he thinks.

Bob is a contemplative hero, but he is far from being humorless. He is in fact a remarkably funny, quick-witted man, with an expansive and ironic comic imagination. That imagination plays most freely in his dreams, which curiously seem more under his guidance and control than the life outside them:

Then I turned over and dreamed on the other side.

I was working in a war plant where a white fellow named Frankie Childs had been killed and the police were there trying to find out who did it.

The police lieutenant said, "We got to find a big tall man with strong arms, big hands, and a crippled leg."

So they started calling in the colored fellows. The first one to be called was a medium-sized, well-built, fast walking, dark brown man of about thirty-five. He was dressed in a faded blue work shirt and blue denim overall pants tied about the waist with a cord. He came up from the basement and walked straight to the lieutenant and looked him in the eye, standing erect and unflinching.

The lieutenant asked, "Can you stand the test?"

"What test?" the colored fellow wanted to know.

"Can you go up to the third floor and look the dead body of Frankie Childs in the face?"

The colored fellow said, "Frankie Childs! Sure,
I can go up and look at that bastard dead or alive."
He had a fine, scholarly voice, carrying but unmusical.
He turned and started up the stairs three at a time.
Suddenly I began to laugh.
        "Oh!" I said to the lieutenant. "You gonna keep
'em running upstairs until you find out what one's
crippled." I fell out and rolled all over the floor
laughing.   (5–6)

Bob is more comical in his dreams than in the real world
because the real world has greater penalties for his wise
cracks. Most of those with whom he comes in contact, Alice
included, barely tolerate his comedy, and because comedy
is so fundamental an ingredient of Bob's character, the in-
tolerance of it becomes a way of denying Bob's existence.

Like *Native Son*, *If He Hollers* contains comic properties without causing laughter. The reader is cut off from
laughing at Bob's jokes by the fact that he cannot laugh at
Bob *as* joke. There is nothing funny in Bob's story. The fact
that he maintains a sense of humor throughout only intensifies the seriousness of his predicament. Moreover, Bob
keeps his humor in check most of the time. Quick retorts
which occur to him continually are choked off, and turn to
hypothetical remarks. In *If He Hollers* comedy is an instrument of perception. It catches life between decision or expectation, and action, and that middle ground is precisely
where Bob lives.

Everybody in the novel is seeking satisfaction of one
kind or another, but nobody gets what he is looking for.
Alice is the high priestess of satisfaction. To her being
satisfied means to gain enough and no more, causing no
offense and taking no risks. Every time Bob seeks her aid or
solace, she stands firm delivering maxims. She asks in-
sincerely how she can help:

        "You can sit up and drink with me until I go blotto,"
I said. "That'll keep me put as long as I stay blotto. Or
you can let me go to bed with you. If I go to sleep
afterward that'll hold me until tomorrow morning—

I don't know for how long after that. . . . Or you can
talk to me, let me talk to you. . . . You can tell me why
you went to Stella's [the lesbian]; how it happened
you went there the first time. . . . I'll tell you everything
I know about myself, about my waking up scared
every morning, about the way I feel toward white
people, why I resent them so goddamned much—
resent the things they can do when all they got is
color—tell you all about what happens inside of me
everytime I go out in the street. . . . Maybe you can
convince me I'm wrong about a lot of things—I've got
an open mind tonight, honestly, baby. . . . Or if you
can't convince me maybe you can make it worth
while for me to try to be different. If I was really sure
about you——" I broke off without finishing,
turned to look at her.   (92)

To which Alice replies, "Bob, your greatest difficulty stems
from your not knowing what you want to do in life" (92).
    What Alice wants Bob to do is to concentrate his
energies, and by concentrate she means shrink his life to so
small a size that it will be barely noticeable. Toward the
end of the novel, before the last scene with Madge, Alice
temporarily wins Bob over with this:

"I must tell you again, Bob darling . . . you need
some definite aim, a goal that you can attain within
the segregated pattern in which we live. . . . I will
admit that we are restricted and controlled in our
economic security, that we have to conform to the
pattern of segregation in order to achieve any manner
of financial success. And I will grant you that we are
subject to racial control in securing education, in
almost all public facilities, welfare, health, hospital-
ization, transportation, in the location of our dwellings,
in all the component parts of our existence that stem
directly or indirectly from economy.

"But, darling, all of life is not commercial. The
best parts of it are not commercial. Love and marriage,
children and homes. Those we control. Our physical
beings, our personal integrity, our private property—

we have as much protection for these as anyone. As
long as we conform to the pattern of segregation we
do not have to fear the seizure of our property
or attack upon our persons.

"And there are many other values that you are
not taking into consideration—spiritual values,
intrinsic values, which are also fundamental com-
ponents of our lives. Honesty, decency, respectability.
Courage—it takes courage to live as a Negro must.
Virtue is our own, to nurture or destroy." (159–160)

Her speech is clearly parody, and in its way, mad, yet Bob
accepts it because he, too, seeks satisfaction. At the end, of
course, Alice's brand of satisfaction is insufficient to save
Bob, and Bob does not remain to satisfy Alice's dreams;
both sets of desires bow to the satisfaction of official justice.

There is no satisfaction for Alice in preaching accommodation, nor is there any for her parents in exemplifying
it. The Harrisons are the sum total of their possessions. Like
Rhobert in *Cane*, they wear their house on their heads.
They can never acquire enough, and are as fearful of losing
social recognition as the turn-of-the-century fictional families of whom they are meant to remind us. Here are fictional parents like those created by Chesnutt, Sutton
Griggs, and J. McHenry Jones, producing a daughter as
well-bred as Regenia Underwood of Jones's *Hearts of Gold*,
a daughter in whom to invest all their hopes of becoming
white. Alice is no accidental name; it evokes the image of
the blonde heroine, pink and white, curtseying and speaking perfect English. In a way, the Harrisons created Alice so
that she might open wonderland to them, not realizing that
they were already living in a wonderland merely by needing
such a wish. No black man, certainly not Bob, of whom
they disapprove, will ever be good enough for their daughter. Before seeing Alice married to Bob, they would prefer
to see her refined out of existence.

Madge remains unsatisfied as well, in every way. She
is unsatisfied sexually because she seeks only sexuality. A
grotesque, gawky figure, men turn from her in disgust. The
other context in which she wishes to be satisfied is her

humiliation of Bob, but she loses there also. Bob's superiors at the plant are not satisfied in their desire to keep Bob in his place. The white workers are not satisfied in their efforts to drive out the black. The black workers are not satisfied with their low positions.

Among them Bob is the least satisfied of all. In college he wanted to be a football star, but he never was. He is not satisfied with his job or the place he lives. Nor is he ever satisfied in love-making. His every attempt at making love in the novel is abortive, by his own design. At the beginning of the story he wants Ella Mae to push him away from her. When he follows Madge to her apartment, the mere sight of her body kills all desire in him. When Alice and he begin to get close, he intentionally brings up the incident at the lesbian's apartment, causing Alice to go cold.

Seeking revenge against Madge, he vacillates, making excuses for inaction. Waiting for the right moment to shoot Stoddart, he hesitates, convincing himself that frightening Stoddart is as good as murder. He continually wishes to crush his enemies, but resorts always to dreams and plotting. The great things he would and should have said fill the novel, and the final irony is that when at last he believes that satisfaction is at hand, he is just about to lose everything: "In the three years in L.A. I'd worked up to a good job in a shipyard, bought a new Buick car, and cornered off the finest colored chick west of Chicago—to my way of thinking. All I had to do was marry her and my future was in the bag. If a black boy couldn't be satisfied with that he couldn't be satisfied with anything" (144). Nothing is created in *If He Hollers*, and nothing sustained. Bob's "Roadmaster," which lets him down at the end by running out of gas, is an obvious symbol of his own unfulfilled promise.

In all of his rantings and suspicions Bob appears to be the archetypal anti-hero: set upon, confused, without direction, angry, contemptuous of material things, wishing to discover his proper place in the universe. Very early in the novel we come to the conclusion that he is exaggerating his plight, often looking for trouble, and that much of the time his woes are created by his own paranoia. Yet the curious aspect of this paranoia is that it does not distort Bob's reality. His craziness is more than equaled by the craziness of the circumstances into which he has stumbled. As Delmore Schwartz observed, "Even paranoids have enemies."

Here is a highly intelligent, keenly sensitive man who has come to the city of the angels in the promised land of California in order to make good. Instead of finding heaven, however, he, like Bigger, with whom he identifies, is shunted from one hell-hole to another. The shipyard itself is hell; overheated, sparks flying everywhere, rivets, everyone soaked with perspiration. To be closeted with Madge at the end is another kind of hell. The prison guard says to Bob, "There ain't anybody to tell—now ain't that hell" (174). And like Bigger, too, Bob lives inside his own head, which eventually produces a hell of various fantasies.

As is the case with every similar unconventional American literary hero, Bob wages war against accommodation. Being black gives him a wider war. In separable instances he may be fighting against the accommodations insisted upon by Alice, Madge, and Stoddart, but what he is ultimately going against is fate:

> Eenie meanie miney mo
> Catch a nigger by the toe
> If he hollers, let him go.
> Out goes Y-O-U.

From the outset of the novel Bob knows that he is a loser, and we know it too. No persecution complex can deny that fact. Moreover, if Bob is crazy, he is never quite as crazy as he would like to be, because to be himself, if crazy, would mean that he was free. It is a waste of his mind to live so fearfully. His story protests against having to protest, against not being allowed to elaborate upon one's own specialness and differences.

No character in all of black fiction is more vital or spirited than this one. Born into a form of anonymity, he has challenged that designation by trying to become an individually identifiable man. His entire story, in fact, is about someone desperate to avoid anonymity, anonymity threatened on all sides by blacks and whites alike. Yet, for all his efforts, at the end of the novel he must join the army, a disciplined institution dependent upon uniformity. He will be given General Issue equipment like everyone else, and he will become anonymous. Nor would it have been any different with Alice, whose aspirations were toward anonymity as well. Bob progresses inevitably in *If He Hollers* from life to non-life, from visibility to invisibility, and his power as a hero only exists for as long as he holds at arm's length his own predetermined disappearance.

The Autobiography of an Ex-Colored Man

The brand of heroism which Bob Jones demonstrates is his persistent struggle against acquiescence. This is true of the majority of black heroes who, like Bob, also disappear as a result of their efforts. Heroes generally contend valiantly against an implacable force without success. The difference in black fiction lies mainly in the manner of losing. Other tragic heroes die or go nobly. These, like Dan Moore walking away, or Big Boy cowering in a truck, or Rufus leaping from a bridge, or Mann, shot in the back, merely depart the scene. As Bob is being led to the induction center, he mutters feebly, "I'm still here," which is only momentarily accurate.

There is another type of black hero, however, who earns his heroism not by fighting his destiny, but by embracing it. He is a hero of internal warfare. Having decided, usually early in his story, to compromise his individuality in accordance with outside expectations, he then begins to deal with the consequences of his decision, his heroism consisting largely of an effort to remember who he is. James Weldon Johnson's *Autobiography of an Ex-Colored Man* is the record of such an effort. If *If He Hollers Let Him Go* illustrates the futility of trying to hold on to one's sense of self, Johnson's novel illustrates the futility of surrendering that sense too easily. Despite the fact that the respective heroes of both novels function according to two opposite kinds of decision, they end up sharing the same anonymous condition.

It is extraordinary that a novel as complicated as *The Autobiography of an Ex-Colored Man* was produced as early as 1912. This was a time when most black authors were engaged in creating stereotypes of black characters in order to counteract other stereotypes which white authors, such as Thomas Dixon, had set before the public. The prevalent theme in black fiction was middle-class upward mobility. The new stereotypes of this post-Reconstruction literature substituted a protest against repression and the caste system for a protest against slavery, yet their ideals were far from egalitarian. Generally these novels were not only anti-Semitic and anti-foreigner; they were anti "low" blacks as well. This attitude was, of course, an apology to the white readers for being black, and the so-called tragic mulatto heroes of the period attained their tragic proportions not because they were caught in the middle, between the black and white worlds, but because they had not quite entered the white one.

The appeal of these novels was primarily to upper- and middle-class whites and middle-class blacks. The literature became popular because it offended no one except those whom the general public of the time had designated as fair game. Certainly the white readers were pleased with their own representations in these books because in the depiction of black troubles, the white characters were almost always exonerated. Either that, or the white villain in question was portrayed as so exceptional in his villainy that he could never be accused of being representative. The novels were made up of stock situations, were populated by stock characters, involved the revelation of stock morality, and were poorly written.

Judged by normal literary standards, the *Autobiography* was a misfit in its era; and yet it is composed of most of the same ingredients as the popular fiction that was produced around it. Except for the final paragraphs of the novel, in which the narrator expresses regret, or more accurately, allows for the possibility of regret, for his decision to pass for white, his story presents the classic "tragic mulatto" situation with all the standard elements. The hero of the narrative tells us at the start that he is writing his autobiography out of a "vague feeling of unsatisfaction, or regret, of almost remorse, from which I am seeking relief (393). He seeks relief because he believes that his story is genuinely tragic, an opinion which comments upon him as much as on his own analyses.

He tells us that he was born in a small town in Georgia shortly after the end of the Civil War, and that soon afterward he moved to Connecticut with his mother, where the two of them lived in "aristocratic" seclusion. His mother and he were supported by money sent regularly by the boy's father, a prominent Southern white man. He tells us how at a young age he became devoted to the piano, how he made his way in school, how he painfully discovered his black heritage, how he learned that his father was white, how he learned to deal with his blackness, how he excelled as a scholar and musician, how he became infatuated with his Sunday School teacher, how he began to discern his own future by studying American history. The first stage of his story closes with his mother's death and his decision to go to college in Atlanta.

The second portion of the narrative consists of a series of losses. As he is about to enter the college in Atlanta he discovers that his tuition money has been stolen. Deciding that a college education is now closed to him, he roves about the South, taking a job in a cigar factory, giving piano lessons, finally determining to head north again, for New York City. There he finds excitement and a new life. He is fascinated by ragtime music, and gets hired as piano player in a night club. There he becomes the favorite of a wealthy white patron who eventually serves as his benefactor.

He accompanies his patron to Europe. Here for the first time he feels freedom. He plans and hopes to become an important black composer, but his patron advises otherwise:

> My boy, you are by blood, by appearance, by
> education, and by tastes a white man. Now, why do

you want to throw your life away amidst the poverty
and ignorance, in the hopeless struggle, of the black
people of the United States? Then look at the terrible
handicap you are placing on yourself by going home
and working as a Negro composer; you can never be
able to get the hearing for your work which it might
deserve. I doubt that even a white musician of
recognized ability could succeed there by working
on the theory that American music should be based
on Negro themes. Music is a universal art; anybody's
music belongs to everybody; you can't limit it to race
or country." (472–473)

At first the narrator disregards this advice, and returns to
the United States in order to pursue his own black culture.
After a number of humiliations observed and felt, however, he makes up his mind to live as a white man. The
Autobiography ends with his marriage to a white woman,
the birth of his children, and this observation: "My love for
my children makes me glad that I am what I am and keeps
me from desiring to be otherwise; and yet, when I sometimes open a little box in which I still keep my fast yellow-
ing manuscripts, the only tangible remnants of a vanished
dream, a dead ambition, a sacrificed talent, I cannot repress
the thought that, after all, I have chosen the lesser part, that
I have sold my birthright for a mess of pottage" (510–511).

　　With the exception of this belated expression of doubt,
the *Autobiography* can pass for a typical period piece.
Throughout the novel there is immense importance
attached to breeding and heredity. It is suggested that if the
hero of the narrative possesses superior qualities of mind
and character, these must be traced to the white side of his
parentage: " 'Well, mother, am I white? Are you white?'
She answered tremblingly: 'No, I am not white, but you—
your father is one of the greatest men in the country—the
best blood of the South is in you—' " (402). It never occurs
to the narrator that his father is in any way to blame for his
difficulties. Both his father and benefactor are frankly
admired for the aristocratic distance they maintain in their
social relations.

The hero also shows contempt for dialect as opposed to proper English. He notes class distinctions among other blacks in order to demonstrate to the middle-class white reader, whose feelings he anticipates, that he fully shares his reader's notion of what constitutes class superiority:

> Washington shows the Negro not only at his best,
> but also at his worst. As I drove around with the
> doctor, he commented rather harshly on those of the
> latter class which we saw. He remarked: "You see
> those lazy, loafing, good-for-nothing darkies; they're
> not worth digging graves for; yet they are the ones
> who create impressions of the race for the casual
> observer. It's because they are always in evidence on
> the street corners, while the rest of us are hard at work,
> and you know a dozen loafing darkies make a bigger
> crowd and a worse impression in this country than
> fifty white men of the same class. But they ought not
> to represent the race. We are the race, and the race
> ought to be judged by us, not by them." (479)

Moreover, he uses a customary divide-and-conquer strategy with his white readers, aiming all the anti-white sentiment expressly at Southern whites, thus fostering an attitude with which the Northern readership cannot help but be pleased. In a long passage on the backwardness of Southern whites he intimates the suggestion that blacks and Northern whites join forces in the name of enlightenment and modernity.

Not only is there nothing in the plot or tone of the *Autobiography* that would have disturbed its audience; there is nothing associated with its author's life or reputation to indicate anything unusual in the book. Johnson issued the *Autobiography* anonymously, and waited fifteen years before affixing his name to the second edition, but by the time of that edition he was a well-known lawyer and had held positions as a career diplomat under Teddy Roosevelt and Wilson. No one would have judged so established a figure and the author of so gentle a race poem as "O Black and Unknown Bards" as capable of producing protest literature. Indeed, by post-Wrightian standards the *Autobiography* is not protest literature at all, but neither is it the apologetic literature it appears to be. In a sense, the novel, like its hero, passes for white, yet, also like its hero, it quietly indicts the white nation, North and South, by its existence.

In the same sense as *If He Hollers Let Him Go*, the *Autobiography* is to a large extent a novel of education. As such, it suggests not only that the hero has learned something by the end of it, principally by way of surviving a number of crises, but that he has also dealt with his growing pains with sufficient perspective to relate the meaning of his story to us. He must have achieved an ordered and relatively complete understanding of his life in order to communicate and interpret it; yet as he tells his story he has to feign a narrative innocence or else reduce his tale to a series of axioms. Since he is a first-person narrator, his vision must always seem to be restricted to the present moment, without predictions of future actions. Nor can anything occur in the novel unless he learns of it himself. He presents us with the same problem as Bob in *If He Hollers:* Is he reliable? To what extent does his reliability or the lack of it shape the book?

The Ex-Colored Man introduces himself to us with this opening:

> I know that in writing the following pages I am divulging the great secret of my life, the secret which for some years I have guarded far more carefully than any of my earthly possessions; and it is a curious study to me to analyse the motives which prompt me to do it. I feel that I am led by the same impulse which forces the un-found-out criminal to take somebody into his confidence, although he knows that the act is likely, even almost certain, to lead to his undoing. I know that I am playing with fire, and I feel the thrill which accompanies that most fascinating pastime; and, back of it all, I think I find a sort of savage and diabolical desire to go gather up all the little tragedies of my life, and turn them into a practical joke on society. (393)

By this brief introduction he defines himself in all his ambiguities. He alludes to his blackness as a guarded secret, placing it in the category either of the best of his earthly possessions or of an extra-terrestrial gift. In either case he gives the impression of being possessed by his possession rather than of being in control of it. Still, although this secret is clearly his own and belongs to him, he refers to himself as a criminal for being in possession of it. On the other hand, he feels the thrill and fascination of being able to divulge it, not out of a desire to unburden his guilty conscience, but out of a feeling of power. He claims that by divulging his secret he will effect his own ruin, and yet he compares his announced confession to a "pastime." And finally, when his reader appreciates that he has built his opening statement to a high pitch of excitement, mounting "thrill" upon "impulse," "fire" upon "thrill," and topping all with "a savage and diabolical desire," he then turns around one more time by reducing this accumulated passion to "little tragedies" and "a practical joke."

What Johnson has done in this first paragraph is to equip his narrator with all the unresolved tensions and vacillations which characterize the entire story. The paragraph consists of three declarative sentences that begin with the assertions "I know," "I feel," "I know." Yet within each of these declarations the narrator reveals that he is not an assertive man. As soon as he has decided to make his bold confession, he simultaneously decides to analyze his motives, and in analyzing those motives he only "thinks" that he finds something "savage and diaboli cal." The truth is that there is nothing savage or diabolical either about his motives or about his manner of describing them. He claims to risk his "undoing," to be "playing with fire," but it is clear that the narrator has strategically protected himself, even while divulging this "greatest secret"; for by saying that he fully expects the worst once his confession is made, he has actually gained the "confidence" of his ally, ourselves. He knows that no decent reader-confessor would ever turn traitor on a privileged communication. He also knows that once it is revealed that the secret he has been guarding is not some heinous crime, but merely skin color, his ally will be so relieved that he will open his heart to this "criminal" forever.

The story of how the Ex-Colored Man becomes a "criminal" begins with a crucial moment of self-recognition. As Janie of *Their Eyes Were Watching God* suddenly saw that she was black in a photograph taken with white children, so the hero of this novel has been forced to recognize the difference in himself. At school he has been made to stand with the black children, apart from the others. That afternoon,

> I rushed up into my own little room, shut the door,
> and went quickly to where my looking-glass hung
> on the wall. For an instant I was afraid to look, but
> when I did, I looked long and earnestly. I had often
> heard people say to my mother: "What a pretty boy
> you have!" I was accustomed to hear remarks about
> my beauty; but now, for the first time, I became
> conscious of it and recognized it. I noticed the ivory
> whiteness of my skin, the beauty of my mouth, the
> size and liquid darkness of my eyes, and how the long,
> black lashes that fringed and shaded them produced
> an effect that was strangely fascinating even to me.
> I noticed the softness and glossiness of my dark hair
> that fell in waves over my temples, making my fore-
> head appear whiter than it really was. How long
> I stood there gazing at my image I do not know. When
> I came out and reached the head of the stairs, I heard
> the lady who had been with my mother going out. I
> ran downstairs and rushed to where my mother
> was sitting, with a piece of work in her hands. I buried
> my head in her lap and blurted out: "Mother, mother,
> tell me, am I a nigger?"   (401)

Mesmerized in the act of self-study, he realizes a duality in his life, the difference between himself as subject and object. At first he seems to be lost in narcissism, but the question he puts to his mother reveals not only the reality behind his thinking, but its brutality as well. He does not ask if he is "colored," or "black," or "Negro." He asks, "Am I a nigger?" thereby staring life, his future, in the face.

From the point of this confrontation he begins to make choices. His fascination before the mirror represents in fact his first choice, because he could choose to see himself physically as either black or white. He chooses to do both. The ensuing choices he makes are either intellectual or intuitive, but all comment on this basic flexibility. Although the heroes of his childhood arc David and Samson, those noted for courage against great odds, the Ex-Colored Man is always searching for more favorable odds, in fact, the sure things. He seeks the easy ways. In the matter of his education he chooses the black college over Harvard or Yale, yet it takes only one set-back to dissuade him from college altogether.

In situations which require action, he steps aside. He confesses that as a boy he preferred to "hide" in his books. After having been robbed of his tuition money, he makes no complaint, nor does he try to retrieve the money. After a shooting in the night club, in which he is circumstantially implicated, he cannot even stomach reading a newspaper account of the event. When he spies his long-lost father in a box at a European opera house, and considers the life to which his father has subjected him, he is caught between weeping and cursing, and does neither. As he witnesses the burning of a fellow black man at the stake, his only response is shame.

He is even cautious with love; he only dares relationships with women when he is certain of his safety. In the early parts of the narrative he describes his first case of puppy love with a certain amusement: "She [his music teacher] of the brown eyes unpacked her violin, and we went through the duet several times. I was soon lost to all other thoughts in the delights of music and love. I saw delights of love without reservation; for at no time of life is love so pure, so delicious, so poetic, so romantic, as it is in boyhood" (412). By the time he has grown up, however, and falls in love seriously, there is the same high melodrama in the account of his handling of it:

Later in the evening she went to the piano and began to play very softly, as if to herself, the opening bars of the Thirteenth Nocturne. I felt that the psychic moment of my life had come, a moment which, if lost, could never be called back; and, in as careless a manner as I could assume, I sauntered over to the piano and stood almost bending over her. She continued playing, but, in a voice that was almost a whisper, she called me by my Christian name and said: "I love you, I love you, I love you." I took her place at the piano and played the Nocturne in a manner that silenced the chatter of the company both in and out of the room, involuntarily closing it with the major triad. (509)

In both passages he uses music to express his feelings, partly because of his basic and somewhat childish romanticism, partly, too, because he is never adamant about his feelings. Like Gabriel Grimes, he is happy to allow signs and symbols to speak on his behalf because he rarely knows what he means to say.

Music itself reveals him. He starts out playing classical piano, then picks up rag. At the same time he feels that rag music is too closely associated with blacks, so he begins to study ways in which classical music may be played like rag. Then he develops his own style in which rag is played classically, shifting continually as he goes from culture to culture, color to color, until eventually he gives up music completely. In point of fact he was never really choosing between black and white music, though he claimed that as his dilemma. He knew from the start that he primarily sought the admiration of a white audience, and the kind of rag he invents is black music filtered through meshes of traditional (white) taste.

He chooses his friends by their appearance of respectability, avoiding contact with blacks generally, except for those who share his own theories of class stratification. When he has the choice of leading or being led, he always picks the latter, as when he set sail for New York, and merely "cast his lot" with those bound for the same destination. A drifter by nature though not an indiscriminate one, he functions as the accompanist on the piano to singers who lead him. And when the strange white benefactor is looking for a companion on his European tour, there is the Ex-Colored Man, ready to be patronized. His final choice is to be black or white, and he makes it with little difficulty.

Each of these choices, of course, defines him. The decisions he makes concerning his education all point to acquiring the kind of education which will not identify him with a particular people. In various choices of taking action, he will not make a move if he risks being singled out or conspicuous. Nor will he venture into romance if there is a chance of his appearing foolish or noticeable. He will not be associated with a specific kind of music, and he will be very careful about the choice of his friends because he does not wish to be connected with a particular kind of people. He will refuse opportunities for leadership out of the fear of becoming prominent. Most significantly, he will choose the absence of color over color because to be colored is to be different, to stand out.

Each of his choices defines him, and each is the wrong choice. Through all of them he reveals himself to be the thoroughly adaptable man, accommodating, at one remove from experience, parasitic and shifty, smooth in self-defense, polished in making the kind of confessions for which there are no penalties; in sum, a fake. Because of all of these things he is not to be trusted, and this is essential to know. It means that his opinions are not to be trusted, his information and tastes are not to be trusted, and most important, neither is his self-esteem or exoneration.

What Johnson did with his Ex-Colored Man was to create a man so completely and obviously out of things (which is why he is identified by being formerly, not presently, something), that he becomes, through his own words, his harshest critic. The Ex-Colored Man is the epitome of the adaptable man. As such he indicts himself, and at the same time his existence indicts the world that encourages or necessitates his adaptability. Like his white benefactor, he is, at the end of his story, as alone as a man can be. He tried to beat the system by disappearing into it, and the success of his strategy may be measured by the absoluteness of the nothing he became.

Invisible Man

That's the end in the beginning, and there's no encore.

—Ralph Ellison, *Invisible Man*

The idea that one day all black men and women may suddenly disappear, either from a certain region or from the face of the earth, has recurred quite often in black writing. In the satire *Black No More* (1931), George Schuyler conceived of a plot in which the "Negro Problem" was solved by "electrical nutrition," a process which changed the texture of the hair, the skin color, and other facial features of black people, thereby making them all white, and disturbing the racial balance of the nation. Kelley's *A Different Drummer* describes a State of the Union from which all blacks depart. Douglas Turner Ward's *Day of Absence* is a play about the same subject: the disappearance of blacks from a Southern town and the ensuing effects on the white population. In Williams' *The Man Who Cried I Am*, Max uncovers an international conspiracy to systematically eliminate the black people of the world.

The different treatments of this theme range from the grim to the hilarious, but each of them is inspired in part by the fear that the disappearance of black Americans is a desirable notion to whites, and that by means of assimilation, isolation, or destruction, it may one day come to pass. The theme is also informed by the fact that most white people do not recognize blacks, do not see them as people. Paradoxically, blacks who wish to be seen by such whites often have to "turn white" or colorless in order to be seen, thereby performing a disappearing act of their own. To evoke literary situations in which black people disappear, then, is a statement of a kind of inner reality despite the seeming exaggeration of the proposition. Moreover, at one point or another almost every black hero seeks to escape from his rut or corner by vanishing, and so becomes an accomplice in his own elimination.

The hero in black fiction who disappears most eloquently is Ralph Ellison's *Invisible Man*. The novel may be categorized a number of ways, but it is above all else the celebration of disappearance, of nothingness. If one takes it as a classical tragedy, the protagonist's flaw lies in his invisibility. If it is read as black comedy, the hero's invisibility is the central sick joke. As a romance, nothing is at the end of the quest; as a bildungsroman, nothing is the product of the education; as a tour de force, nothing is the vehicle. The hero progresses from South to North to nothing; from capitalism to communism to nihilism. He makes a long and arduous pilgrimage which finishes in a basement; he starts out heading for the future, and settles down in the nineteenth century; he begins life believing in a network of illusions, and ends as an illusion himself, describing his invisibility to those who cannot see him, and, in addressing his narrative to white people, explaining himself to those who made him, or wish him to remain, inexplicable.

In terms of the cyclical conception of the literature generally, Ellison's hero represents the ultimate stage. As an illusion himself, he is connected to a view of American history which tends to make illusions heroic, a cycle which moves from promise to reality to illusion, and back to implicit promise. In the beginning the nation was all promise: the American Revolution would be ethical as well as political. There were no limits to the land, or to natural resources, or to the capabilities of the individual. Soon realities set in: there were limits to the land; there was a slave foundation to the economy, and so forth. "The contradiction between noble ideals and the actualities of our conduct generated a guilt," Ellison wrote elsewhere, "an unease of spirit, from the very beginning, and . . . the American novel at its best has always been concerned with this basic predicament" (*Shadow and Act*).

Out of this predicament, out of the collision between

The Hero Vanishes   185

promise and reality, certain illusions were conjured up. Encouraged by Hollywood and politics, the function of such illusions was to persuade ourselves that certain deficiencies, realities, did not exist. The ideal of American heroism was itself such an illusion. This is what the creation of the Invisible Man points to. The hero in fiction who is an illusion himself is saying something by this fact alone. He is not merely anti-heroic in the conventional sense, but anti false heroism, and by proclaiming his condition, he is also expressing an attitude which is critical of other American heroes who may appear to be more substantial than he, but are not. In a way, his declaration of invisibility gives him true heroic stature, because he makes something, himself, out of nothing.

He begins his narrative by stating simply, "I am an invisible man." Ishmael introduced himself by name, but this man, having no name, identifies himself as unidentifiable. In the essay "Hidden Name and Complex Fate," Ellison said that it is through our names that we first place ourselves in the world. By announcing his namelessness the Invisible Man announces that he has no particular place. Initially this was Ellison's own announcement as well. Named for Ralph Waldo Emerson, he described (in "Hidden Name") the process of growing into his famous name, of rejecting it originally because it was imposed upon him, then eventually embracing it when he began to reach some moral conclusions of his own, and to get a glimpse of who he was or might become. His Invisible Man remains unnamed, however, meaning either that even by the conclusion of his journey he has not discovered an identification, or that namelessness is itself his name, his identity lying in the indefinite and exploratory. Curiously, unlike the Ex-Colored Man, whose account is far more reasonable, he is a most believable and trustworthy narrator. Being nothing himself, he has nothing to gain by distortion, and nothing to lose by the truth.

The story he tells us is that he lives in an apartment house otherwise occupied by whites, in a section of the basement "shut off and forgotten during the nineteenth century" (9). His apartment is lit by 1,369 light bulbs which he has wired to his ceiling. He entertains himself by playing his radio-phonograph. He particularly likes to listen to Louis Armstrong's "Black and Blue," because Armstrong "made poetry out of being invisible" (11). He acknowledges that he is in hiding, but describes his state as "hibernation," which is a "covert preparation for a more overt action" (16). He does not say what form that action will take, but immediately launches into his biography, demonstrating a familiarity with or power over the reader, like the Ancient Mariner's, which compels us to listen. By alternatively accusing, taunting, sympathizing, and agreeing with us he forces our recognition of his life, which is a recognition of the invisible. He also suggests that since we participated in his life, and partly shaped it, we ought to be interested in hearing about it.

As a high school senior the Invisible Man was class valedictorian, and his senior oration was so impressive that he was invited to deliver it again before the white citizens of his Southern town. At a local businessman's smoker he is made to strip to the waist and put on boxing gloves, and is led onto a stage with other black boys. There a stark naked blonde with a small American flag tattooed on her stomach is beginning to dance. The black boys are threatened by the onlookers whether they stare at the blonde or not. Then they are blindfolded and are thrown into a battle royal, a free-for-all fist fight with one another. Afterward, the white men toss coins to them on an electrified carpet. Finally, the Invisible Man is asked to give his speech to the jeering audience. When he finishes, there is mock "thunderous applause," and a gift for him of a calfskin briefcase. That night he dreams he is with his dead grandfather at the circus. The old man tells him to open an envelope in his briefcase. The message reads: "To Whom It May Concern, Keep this Nigger-Boy Running" (35).

He attends a prominent black college (Tuskegee) on a scholarship awarded him by the white community. He seeks to become another Booker T. Washington. When Mr. Norton, the most important white trustee of the college, makes his yearly visit, the Invisible Man is assigned to drive the man around. His assignment is an honor, but he makes the mistake of getting lost on the road and takes Norton into the back country, away from the campus. There Norton meets Trueblood, a black farmer whose daughter is now pregnant with his own child. Trueblood is surprised to report that white people have treated his family very well since the incident: "What I don't understand is how I done the worst thing a man can do in his own family and 'stead of things gettin' bad, they got better. The niggers up at the school don't like me, but the white folks treats me fine" (65). Norton, who indicates incestuous feelings about his own daughter, gives Trueblood a hundred dollars.

He has been shaken by this encounter, and asks the Invisible Man to drive him somewhere for a drink. The only place nearby is a roadhouse called the Golden Day, and the afternoon when Norton and the Invisible Man arrive is the time when the inmates of a local veterans hospital are scheduled to call on the prostitutes who work in the roadhouse. Norton is mortified. A brawl erupts in which the inmates gang up on their supervisor, Supercargo (Superego). These inmates have all come from the black middle class. Their leader and spokesman is a former surgeon, now a madman, who was driven from his profession by his white colleagues. Norton is terrified by the fracas, and faints. The Invisible Man asks if he is dead; "DEAD!" says the surgeon indignantly. "He *caint* die!" (89).

When the two of them return to the college, Norton leaves the Invisible Man, advising him, in an absent-minded way, to study Emerson. The Invisible Man is petrified at the prospect of how Dr. Bledsoe, the ruthless and pragmatic college president, will respond to the day's blunders. Waiting for Bledsoe's judgment he attends an address at chapel by the Reverend Homer Barbee (Homer) who deifies the "Founder" of the college, and exhorts the congregation to "aspire, each of you, to some day follow in his footsteps. Great deeds are yet to be performed" (120). After the address, Bledsoe calls the Invisible Man before him, and expels him from the college. The Invisible Man threatens to expose Bledsoe as a liar and cynic, but Bledsoe tells him that his arms are too short to box with him. Nevertheless, as an apparent gesture of kindness, he gives the Invisible Man seven letters of introduction to powerful men in New York with whom he may find work. After a suitable period of suspension, Bledsoe says, the Invisible Man may return to school.

In New York the Invisible Man soon discovers that Bledsoe's letters of reference are in actuality letters of condemnation that say, in effect, "Keep this nigger-boy running." There is no hope that he will be allowed to return to school. He takes a job in the Liberty Paint Factory, whose company slogan is "Keep America Pure with Liberty Paints," and whose most celebrated product is a paint called "Optic White." The Invisible Man is told that the secret of the paint's special whiteness is that ten drops of black paint are stirred into the white solution until they disappear. The secret formula of the paint is maintained by the black foreman of the factory, Lucius Brockway, to whom the Invisible Man is assigned. Brockway is an Uncle Tom and the backbone of the industry. He and the Invisible Man fight; there is an immense explosion; and the Invisible Man lands in the factory hospital. Here he is symbolically reborn. When he can no longer remember anything of his past, he is pronounced cured.

Moving to Harlem, he becomes involved in the "Brotherhood," an organization similar to the Communist Party. He delivers a spontaneous speech at a street demonstration against an eviction, and draws the attention of the Party members. He is told that "history is born in your brain," and becomes a professional orator and agitator for the Brotherhood, made privy to its secrets, and assigned to Harlem. But just as his success mounts and the movement he inspires reaches its peak, the Brotherhood decides to switch its ideological direction and desert the cause of blacks. The Invisible Man discovers that the one-eyed Party leader, Brother Jack, has manipulated him. He has been forced to sacrifice his individuality for the Party, but

The Hero Vanishes   189

when he begins to doubt the Party itself, he realizes that he is as invisible as ever. He is presented with a slave's leg chain by Brother Tarp as a link to his past and future.

The final encounter of the book takes place between the Invisible Man and Ras the Destroyer. Ras is the black nationalist who seeks to drive the Brotherhood out of Harlem. His name is the word for an Ethiopian prince. In a street fight, another battle royal, Ras takes on the Invisible Man, along with his young aide, Tod Clifton. When Ras gets the advantage of Tod, however, he is unable to kill his fellow black man. Later Tod (in German, death) descends to a personal abyss. Filled with self-hate, he peddles cupie dolls, "Sambo the Dancing Doll," his own effigy. He is shot to death by a policeman for resisting arrest on a misdemeanor. The Invisible Man takes flight, and is hounded by Ras as a traitor to his people.

Pursued into a drug store one evening, he disguises himself with a pair of dark glasses and a wide-brimmed hat. Immediately everyone takes him to be a certain "Mr. Rinehart." People begin to greet him as Rinehart, who is evidently a master confidence man. The Invisible Man, thinking that he has discovered an ideal new identity, wonders, "Could he be all of them: Rine the runner and Rine the gambler and Rine the briber and Rine the lover and Rinehart the Reverend? Could he himself be both rind and heart?" (430). Through his new glasses he sees clearly for the first time that Rinehart's multiple identities might be the answer of how to live: "His world was possibility and he knew it. He was years ahead of me and I was a fool. I must have been crazy and blind. The world in which we lived was without boundaries. A vast seething, hot world of fluidity, and Rine the rascal was at home" (430).

In the Harlem race riot which ends the novel, the Invisible Man discards his Rinehart disguise, but maintains his faith in the idea that some form of invisibility is the way for him to survive. Acknowledging that he is not strong enough to do battle against the Brotherhood or Ras, he withdraws from everything. In a dream sequence he is trapped by Ras, who threatens to lynch him. The Invisible

Man grabs the spear which Ras has been wielding and hurls it through Ras's cheeks and mouth, thus silencing the Ras within himself. In the end, he is chased by a gang of white men armed with baseball bats, and he leaps into a coal cellar where he cannot be seen. His final dream is of his own castration. His tormenters ask, "How does it feel to be free of illusion," to which he responds, "Painful and empty" (493).

Ellison called the blues "an art of ambiguity, an assertion of the irrepressibly human over circumstance." The solo in a jazz band specifically is an assertion of the individual at once within and against the group as a whole. Such an act of assertion is what the Invisible Man attempts continually, but the difficulty is that his groups keep changing. Inevitably his various self-assertions become anachronistic or otherwise misplaced because all of the groups to which he belongs eventually turn and conspire against him. He is told that academic success will serve him well among whites, but discovers symbolically at the battle royal that the rewards of the American success story are not for black boys. He seeks love from the white townspeople, but instead receives pain and ridicule particularly because he did seek love, attempting to accommodate himself to that which would have no part of him under any conditions.

When he believed he would receive honor, he was given terror and confusion in the sight of the naked blonde. When he thought he would receive money, he was given an electric shock. When the audience was supposed to praise his oration, they jeered. When he thought they would jeer more loudly at the end, they applauded. When he thought he would suffer further humiliation at the close of the evening, he received his briefcase and scholarship. The scholarship, which he then trusts to be his passport to happiness, leads him to disappointment and degradation.

The same shifts occur in college, when he is assigned to serve as Norton's chauffeur. He wants desperately to do well by doing what is expected of him, but only seems able to get into trouble. It is not the Invisible Man, but Trueblood, whom Norton rewards, and he does so partly because Trueblood has committed the sin which Norton sought to commit, because in a sense Trueblood has gone to hell for them both; but also because Trueblood has behaved as Norton secretly wishes a black man to behave. The Invisible Man is confused; the good are expelled from college, and the wicked are given a hundred dollars.

He would redeem himself still, but redemption is forbidden. He accommodates himself to his period of probation, but discovers through Bledsoe's letters that he has not been on probation, that he has been expelled from the start. He accommodates himself to the industrial life, but another black man, who is a professional accommodator, beats him down. He tries to accommodate himself to the Brotherhood, and to succeed there, but is told that one of his speeches showed "too much feeling," and that he needs to learn to conduct his life more strictly. When he escapes from the Brotherhood, and later from Ras as well, he escapes into nowhere and nothing, having found the one context of accommodation where he is most free.

Up to the point of this final accommodation he has been asserting himself not only against groups of people but against certain abstract ideas as well. Like most black heroes, he has had a great deal of trouble with the conception of time: with being on time for appointments, with knowing when his time has come. In his first words to us, he talks of how he admires Louis Armstrong's sense of timing, which eventually becomes the Invisible Man's own sense: "Sometimes you're ahead and sometimes behind. Instead of the swift and imperceptible flowing of time, you are aware of its nodes, those points where time stands still or from which it leaps ahead. And you slip into the breaks and look around. That's what you hear vaguely in Louis' music" (11). He describes a prize fight between a fancy boxer and a "yokel," which the yokel won because he "had simply stepped inside his opponent's sense of time" (12). This is what the Invisible Man learns to do with his own opponents, because he has been shut out of the white man's time. (When Trueblood attacked his daughter, he was dreaming of a white lady trying to keep him out of a grandfather clock.) At the start of his career, the Invisible Man wants to buy a watch. At his castration, he "lost all sense of time," and began to develop a new one.

He has also had to assert himself against recorded time, against history. The battle royal itself is a historical exercise, encompassing the national desire for spectacle, for glory (the flag), for beauty (the blonde), for temptation and abstinence, for violence and war (the fighting boys), for wealth (the coins on the carpet), for reward of virtue (the briefcase), and for the sentimental and platitudinous in the protagonist's speech. The Invisible Man wishes to become an important part of history, but the only historical association made available to him is slavery: the statue of the slave on display in his museum; the gift of the leg chain, which he cannot discard. The Brotherhood offers a different kind of slavery. Brother Jack raises a toast "to History and to Change" (269), but he brings no change to the Invisible Man. History merely repeats itself in the episode where one of the women in the Brotherhood disrobes before the hero, at once seducing him and insuring his loyalty to the Party, in a more sophisticated version of the striptease at the battle royal.

When the Invisible Man sees Tod Clifton hawking his cupie dolls, he asks himself, "Why should a man deliberately plunge outside of history and peddle an obscenity?" (379). When he sees Tod gunned down and returns to Harlem, he looks upon his own people as if for the first time: "They'd been there all along, but somehow I'd missed them even when my [Brotherhood] work had been most successful. They were outside the groove of history, and it was my job to get them in, all of them" (383). This he could not do, because history is cyclical, and his people are in it, even when they stand outside of it. Before making a great speech for the Brotherhood he notices the photograph of a former prize-fight champion who had lost his sight in the ring, just as he in the battle royal had also been unable to see, as he is unable to see now under the floodlights, in a boxing ring, waiting to make yet another speech to earn the white man's approval.

He goes up against history, and he contends fate as well. Numbers and cards work against him; he tells his landlady that his number is up; there are seven letters of introduction. Norton is continually talking about destiny. He says, "I had a feeling that your people were somehow connected with my destiny" (42), meaning that he simply saw how his (the nation's) future and past were related to the treatment of blacks. He cites Emerson as having had a hand in the black man's destiny. The Invisible Man's destiny is less theoretical, however. He learns his fate in his grandfather's message to him and in his various expulsions. As a "nigger-boy," he only stops running when he disappears.

As in *Native Son*, there are a number of forms of blindness in the novel, and the Invisible Man, by always trying to see things clearly and accurately, is asserting himself against this force as well. When Norton's eyes are closed he resembles a terrifying ghost or god. Homer Barbee is blind spiritually and physically, as is Brother Jack (one-eyed Jack), despite his one good eye, which makes him look like a Cyclops. The Invisible Man wants to be different from these men, but he is threatened by blindness all around him. At one point he says, "I was no Samson" (212), suggesting that having lost his strength, he might be blinded. At another he confronts a man singing about a lady who had "feet like a monkey, legs like a maaad bull-dog" (156). A sphinx-like creature, she both suggests to the Invisible Man that life is ambiguous, and indicates the hero's kinship to Oedipus. He is temporarily blinded by the spotlight when he delivers his oration for the Brother-hood, and the speech itself is on blind mice. Moreover, it is presented to those as blind as he, the blind leading the blind.

The theme of blindness in *Invisible Man* is connected to other problems of vision. The Founder of the college was hailed as a visionary; yet the nature of the college shows how limited his vision was. There is a veil on the face of the statue of the slave, and it is impossible to tell if the veil is about to come off or go on. The "Optic White" color, which is the pride and fortune of Liberty Paints, is manufactured expressly for national monuments, effecting a national whitewash. The way people have chosen to see the country, or the world, as entirely white, is an optical illusion. The Invisible Man himself progresses toward becoming an optical illusion, with the distinction that "I'm invisible, not blind" (498), that at the end he is able to see himself clearly in invisibility, a way of saying to the reader that if you cannot see me, the optical defect is yours.

The Invisible Man is also asserting himself against madness, his own and the madness of those about him. During the melee in the Golden Day, Supercargo shouts, "I WANT ORDER!" (77), which is the Invisible Man's own cry, but the veterans go wild and create chaos instead. The Golden Day has actually devolved into a madhouse, having been at various points in its past a church, a bank, a restaurant, a gambling house, and a whorehouse. Its history implies that the nation's history has also tended toward madness. Surveying his life, the Invisible Man wonders, "What if history itself were a madman?" (381). There is chaos in the Harlem race riot, and in the personality of Rinehart, who is at once all things and nothing. The Invisible Man seeks cohesion, but the apparent order of the college masks its disorder, and the "discipline" of the Brotherhood hides hysteria. He is continually losing his bearings and control, and even when he gets hold of himself at the end, the tone of his narrative is borne by the terribly precise language of the mad.

He starts out wanting to become a leader. He is told by Norton that he should read Emerson, and is embarrassed by the fact that he had not yet done so; yet, although he does not know it, his initial optimism is based upon the attitude spread abroad by such documents as "Self-Reliance," on the conviction that "we are now men, and must accept in the highest mind the same transcendental destiny; and not minors and invalids in a protected corner, not cowards fleeing before a revolution, but guides, redeemers and benefactors, obeying the Almighty effort and advancing on Chaos and the Dark." The Invisible Man believes that this is all possible for him, and when he eventually discovers that those who were advancing on chaos and the dark were advancing on him, his problem is to determine who exactly has gone crazy, the nation or himself. In the novel the twentieth-century Mr. Emerson, the son of one of those to whom Bledsoe refers the hero, has become an importer of curios who no longer deals in American goods. It is he who reveals the contents of Bledsoe's letter, but he has no other substantial courage, describing himself as a prisoner of his father, who runs him, the business, and a great deal else.

Nevertheless, despite its abuse, the idea of self-reliance is what sustains the Invisible Man throughout all of his mishaps. It is the abuse, not the idea itself, which is faulted, and in a sense the Invisible Man uses his own chaotic and dark existence to prove the principle. By acknowledging and celebrating his invisibility, he declares that he will now use it in an effort to begin life over again, confronting fate with fate, which is also an Emersonian idea. After all of his various assertions, he tells us that come the spring thaw he will end his hibernation, and emerge from his basement. His final assertion is invisibility itself, the act of knowing that one is nothing. Equipped with this creed, he will once more tackle the world, demonstrating the assertion of the irrepressibly human over circumstance.

The Invisible Man is the epitome of the self-conscious. He verifies the Hegelian idea that one *is* only by being acknowledged and recognized, and therefore depends heavily on our understanding and sympathy. He declares to us that in invisibility there is substance, the way Aichinger's "Bound Man" celebrates freedom in being tied up, Kafka's "Hunger Artist" eats heartily during starvation, and the occupant of Sartre's "Room" enjoys limitless expanses. Yet, if the Invisible Man emerges from his basement, in what ways will he be better off than at the outset of his story? He often notes that in the end is the beginning.

The observation applies to himself because the point is that as a black man he was always an invisible man. Indeed, it was his efforts to make himself seen which got him into difficulties. If he had remained inconspicuous, had not taken the wrong turns or made the wrong speeches, he might have thrived. Now he hopes to thrive on invisibility, yet there is no evidence that this will happen. All of his former assertions ended in nothing, and there is no reason to suppose that by connecting nothing with nothing he will fare any better this time.

Of course, he may fare better in terms of self-appraisal. No matter who his future pursuers turn out to be, at least he will no longer be burdened with great expectations and confidence. His fall from promise to reality will not be as steep as it had been before, and he is better able to recognize the enemies around him. Most of all, he has managed to produce an important social document in his memoirs. Still, as for his final hopeful words, that "there's a possibility that even an invisible man has a socially responsible role to play" (503), therein may lie an illusion even greater than the illusion of his being. For he will assuredly not come back into society as Jesus walked in the Grand Inquisitor section of *The Brothers Karamazov*, softly, unobserved, yet recognized by everyone. Inversely, the Invisible Man will be observed by all, and recognized by no one. He is not actually invisible after all, but black, and his new self-awareness, his experience and resolve will not change that.

Irving Howe has observed that in the twentieth century the underground man comes into his own. He plumbs the depths of his own infinitely paradoxical nature, and surfaces with enough personal schisms to keep himself going forever. This is what the Invisible Man tells us at the end: that he will continue to live and try to make coherent sense of his life and the life around him. He is less spiteful than Dostoevsky's underground man, who winds up cursing the underground, but like his literary predecessor, he is determined to survive his fate. "In the man of color there is the constant effort to run away from his own individuality," said Fanon, "to annihilate his own presence." The Invisible Man by annihilating his presence has asserted his individuality, and as long as he keeps that assertion to himself he will be all right. Only when he exposes his individuality, his invisibility, to public scrutiny will he be in danger, because the world upstairs has proven that it can make nothing even out of nothing, if the nothing is black. When the Invisible Man comes up for air, he will be a hero, and he will be gone.

Blyden Jackson ("The Negro's Negro in Negro Literature") makes the point that the hero in black fiction is virtually always the same man, that "whether as tragic mulatto, or bel-esprit, or bogeyman or artist manqué, he is still Big Boy leaving home." Whether or not this is wholly true, it is certainly demonstrable that most black heroes proceed in a cycle and reach the same end. The moral imperative of *Invisible Man* is: recognize the invisible; yet by the time most of the heroes of black fiction have completed their stories, recognition is not easy. Mann, An' Sue, and Cross Damon wind up shot to death. Silas is incinerated in his home. Bigger is locked away. Big Boy is hidden in the back of a truck. Bessie is faceless. The Ex-Colored Man is white. Bob Jones will be indistinguishable in his army uniform, or perhaps dead. John Grimes may resemble his father. Richard has slit his wrists. Sandy is lost in the city. Rufus is under water. Cooley fades back into Harlem. Jake has run from Harlem. Ray sails away. And the Invisible Man has disappeared altogether.

Most heroes die in one way or another at the end of their adventures, so there is nothing special about the fact that these particular ones do likewise. It is not their various deaths which give black heroes their tragic stature, but the fact that in retrospect their lives seem to have made so small an impression on their worlds. We devotedly follow the trials of an individual hero up to and into his final glorious or inglorious defeat; yet afterward it seems in most instances that the character has never been, that he or she had only been beating the air all along. It took a couple of killings for Bigger Thomas to make a name for himself, yet one knows that even Bigger's spectacular life will have changed nothing. As for a hero like the Invisible Man, who merely tried to think his way to achievement, there will be no memory of him whatsoever.

The patterns in black fiction are cyclical, enclosed and self-sufficient. The hostile world or nation leaves its mark on its characters, but try as they may, the characters do not reciprocate. The certainty of a hero's entrapment gives him a certain strength, but it also peters him out, and therefore, when he has reached the end of his efforts, after starting out on a circular track, after attempting to change direction by means of his youth, education, love, or humor, or by trying to escape into his own elusive and vague history, after discovering in the failure of all such attempts that the world which has caused all this failure is not only unattainable but undesirable, the hero vanishes. He starts out wishing to be free, and realizes his freedom in self-disintegration.

Works Cited

Baldwin, James. *Another Country.* New York: Dell Publishing Co., 1962.

——— *The Fire Next Time.* New York: Dial Press, 1963.

———*Go Tell It on the Mountain.* New York: Grosset and Dunlap, 1952.

———*Notes of a Native Son.* Boston: Beacon Press, 1963.

——— "Sonny's Blues." In *Going to Meet the Man.* New York: Dial Press, 1965.

Bone, Robert A. *The Negro Novel in America.* New Haven: Yale University Press, 1968.

Bontemps, Arna. *Black Thunder.* New York: Macmillan, 1936.

———*God Sends Sunday.* New York: Harcourt Brace, 1931.

Brown, Cecil. *The Life and Loves of Mr. Jiveass Nigger.* Greenwich, Conn.: Fawcett, 1969.

Brown, Claude. *Manchild in the Promised Land.* New York: New American Library, 1965.

Brown, Sterling A. "Negro Character as Seen by White Authors." In *Dark Symphony: Negro Literature in America,* ed. James A. Emanuel and Theodore L. Gross. New York: The Free Press, 1968.

Chase, Richard. *The American Novel and Its Tradition.* Garden City, N.Y.: Doubleday and Co., 1957.

Chesnutt, Charles. *The House Behind the Cedars.* Boston and New York: Houghton Mifflin, 1900.

Cullen, Countee. *One Way to Heaven.* New York and London: Harper, 1932.

Demby, William. *Beetlecreek.* New York: Rinehart, 1950.

Dubois, W. E. B. *The Souls of Black Folk.* In *Three Negro Classics.* New York: Avon Books, 1968.

Dunbar, Paul L. *The Fanatics.* New York: Dodd, Mead, 1901.

———*The Love of Landry.* New York: Dodd, Mead, 1900.

——— *The Sport of the Gods.* New York: Dodd, Mead, 1902.

——— *The Uncalled.* New York. Dodd, Mead, 1898.

——— "We Wear the Mask." In *Dark Symphony: Negro Literature in America,* ed. James A. Emanuel and Theodore L. Gross. New York: The Free Press, 1968.

Ellison, Ralph. "Flying Home." In *Dark Symphony: Negro Literature in America,* ed. James A. Emanuel and Theodore L. Gross. New York: The Free Press, 1968.

———"Hidden Name and Complex Fate." In *Shadow and Act.* New York: Random House, 1964.

——— *Invisible Man.* New York: New American Library, 1952.

Fanon, Frantz. *Black Skin, White Masks.* New York: Grove Press, 1967.

———— *The Wretched of the Earth*. New York: Grove Press, 1968.

Gaines, Ernest J. "The Sky Is Gray." In *Bloodline*. New York: Dial Press, 1968.

Griggs, Sutton E. *The Hindered Hand*. Nashville, Orion, 1905.

Himes, Chester. *If He Hollers Let Him Go*. New York: New American Library, 1971.

Hughes, Carl M. *The Negro Novelist*. New York: Citadel Press, 1953.

Hughes, Langston. *The Best of Simple*. New York: Hill and Wang, 1961.

———— ed. *The Book of Negro Humor*. New York: Dodd, Mead, 1966.

———— *Not Without Laughter*. New York: Knopf, 1963.

———— *Simple Speaks His Mind*. New York: Simon and Schuster, 1950.

———— *Simple's Uncle Sam*. New York: Hill and Wang, 1967.

Hurston, Zora Neale. *Their Eyes Were Watching God*. Greenwich, Conn.: Fawcett, 1969.

Jackson, Blyden. "The Negro's Negro in Negro Literature." In *Black Literature in America*, ed. Raman K. Singh and Peter Fellowes. New York: Crowell, 1970.

Johnson, James W. *The Autobiography of an Ex-Colored Man*. In *Three Negro Classics*. New York: Avon Books, 1965.

———— "O Black and Unknown Bards." In *Dark Symphony: Negro Literature in America*, ed. James A. Emanuel and Theodore L. Gross. New York: The Free Press, 1968.

Jones, J. McHenry. *Hearts of Gold*. Wheeling, W. Va.: Daily Intelligencer Steam Job Press, 1896.

Jones, LeRoi. *Home*. New York: William Morrow, 1966.

———— "Philistinism and the Negro Writer." In *Anger and Beyond*, ed. Herbert Hill. New York: Harper and Row, 1966.

———— "A Poem for Willie Best." In *The Dead Lecturer*. New York: Grove Press, 1964.

Kelley, William M. *dem*. New York: Doubleday, 1967.

———— *A Different Drummer*. New York: Doubleday, 1962.

Marshall, Paule. *Soul Clap Hands and Sing*. New York: Atheneum, 1961.

McCall, Dan. *The Example of Richard Wright*. New York: Harcourt, Brace and World, 1969.

McKay, Claude. *Banana Bottom*. New York: Harper, 1933.

———— *Banjo*. New York: Harper, 1929.

———— *Home to Harlem*. New York: Harper, 1928.

McPherson, James A. "A Matter of Vocabulary." In *Hue and Cry*. Boston: Atlantic–Little Brown, 1969.

Petry, Ann. *Country Place*. Boston: Houghton Mifflin, 1947.

———— *The Street*. Boston: Houghton Mifflin, 1946.

Schuyler, George S. *Black No More: Being an Account of the Strange and Wonderful Workings of Science in the Land of the Free, A.D. 1933–1940.* New York: Macauley, 1931.

Thurman, Wallace. *The Blacker the Berry.* New York: Macauley, 1929.

Toomer, Jean. *Cane.* New York: Harper and Row, 1969.

———— *Essentials.* Chicago: Lakeside Press, 1931.

———— *The Flavor of Man.* Philadelphia: The Young Friends Movement, 1949.

———— *York Beach.* In *The New American Caravan,* ed. Alfred Kreymborg, Lewis Mumford, and Paul Rosenfeld. New York: Macauley, 1929.

Ward, Douglas T. *Day of Absence.* New York: Avon, 1970.

Warshow, Robert. "The Legacy of the 30's." In *The Immediate Experience,* ed. Lionel Trilling. New York: Atheneum, 1971.

Weidman, Jerome. "My Father Sits in the Dark." In *Firsts of the Famous,* ed. Whit Burnett. New York: Ballantine Books, 1962.

White, Walter. *Flight.* New York: Grosset and Dunlap, 1926.

Williams, John A. *The Man Who Cried I Am.* Boston: Little, Brown, 1967.

Wright, Richard. "Almos' a Man." In *Eight Men.* Cleveland: World, 1961.

———— *Black Boy.* Cleveland: World, 1961.

———— "The Literature of the Negro in the United States." In *White Man, Listen!* New York: Doubleday, 1957.

———— *Native Son.* New York: Harper and Row, 1966.

———— *The Outsider.* New York: Harper, 1953.

———— *Uncle Tom's Children.* New York: Harper and Row, 1965.

Index

Index   209